Is God a Christian?

Is God a

Christian?

Creating a Community of Conversation

R. KIRBY GODSEY

Mercer University Press
Macon, Georgia

MUP/H825
MUP/H825e

First Edition.

Books published by Mercer University Press are
printed on acid free paper that meets the
requirements of American National Standard
for Information Sciences—Permanence of Paper
for Printed Library Materials.

Mercer University Press is a member of Green
Press initiative (greenpressinitiative.org), a
nonprofit organization working to help
publishers and printers increase their use of
recycled paper and decrease their use of fiber
derived from endangered forests. This book is
printed on recycled paper.

978-0-88146-242-5 | H825 | Hardback
978-0-88146-248-7 | H825e | ebook

*Library of Congress
Cataloging-in-Publication Data*

Godsey, R. Kirby (Raleigh Kirby), 1936-
  Is God a Christian? / R. Kirby Godsey. — 1st ed.
    p. cm.
  Includes bibliographical references and index.
  ISBN 978-0-88146-242-5 (hardcover : alk.
paper) — ISBN 978-0-88146-248-7 (e-book)
  1. God. 2. Christianity and other religions.
3. Religions—Relations. I. Title.
  BL473.G58 2011
  261.2—dc22

2011003172

Book design by Burt&Burt

MERCER
UNIVERSITY PRESS

Endowed by
TOM WATSON BROWN
and
THE WATSON-BROWN FOUNDATION, INC.

BOOKS BY R. KIRBY GODSEY

When We Talk about God, Let's Be Honest (1996; repr. 2006)

Centering Our Souls: Devotional Reflections of a University President (2005)

Courage Factor: A Collection of Presidential Essays (2005)

With Walter B. Shurden and William D. Underwood:
*Baptist Summit at Mercer University: 19-20 January 2006,
Three Addresses* (2006)

Inaugural Festschrift for President Godsey, edited by Ben C. Fisher:
New Pathways: A Dialogue in Christian Higher Education (1980)

Is God a

Christian?

CONTENTS

In a world composed of almost seven billion people, about 2.2 billion of them claim to be Christian. And while Christianity is continuing to grow at a modest rate, other religions are growing at a faster pace. Some scholars predict that Islam will overtake Christianity as the world's largest religion by the end of the twenty-first century. Predictions aside, religions are competing for the world stage and, in the competition, Christians seem certain that God is on their side.

Christians often think and behave as though God were a Christian. Most Christians assume that Christianity is the one and only religion that is God-inspired and that carries the imprimatur of God's blessing. I am asking if that assumption is true by encouraging us to examine more honestly our own faith and by considering more openly and less judgmentally the faiths that inspire others. The world has grown too small and the stakes for mankind have grown too high for any of us to engage our faith as if our understanding of God represents the only way God's presence may be known in the world.

On the face of it, the answer to the question of whether God is a Christian seems quite easy for those who say "yes" as well as for those who say "no." For those who say "yes," it is unthinkable and perhaps even frightening or disorienting to entertain the notion that God does not solely belong to the Christian tradition. God is a Christian because we have come to know God as a Christian. Similarly for those who say "no," it is equally implausible to identify God as a Christian because their experience of God has been mediated through radically different traditions. In short, God is not a Christian because they have experienced God as "Allah" or as "Yahweh." Furthermore, the numbers are telling: most of God's human creation are not Christian. Therefore, the conflicts among us and within us are not abstractions. These conflicts are "in your face" clashes, visceral and compelling.

Only a few years ago, I watched and listened as a majority Christian body in the city of Atlanta vigorously voted, with steamy resentment and not even half-hidden hostility, to exclude a fellow Christian church from its association because that autonomous congregation embraced gays and lesbians as Christian brothers and sisters who should be accorded all the rights of fellowship and holy communion. The rhetoric was loud, ugly, and condescending. I walked from that "Christian" gathering wanting to bathe away the residue of the poisoned air that hung in the room like urban smog.

Then, in that same year, I gazed as if in a trance at the gaping, cavernous wound in New York City where the Twin Towers of the World Trade Center had stood. Nine months earlier, I had sat on the 104th floor having lunch, captured by the breathtakingly dramatic views of Manhattan. On this day, however, I stood in the cold and recalled watching in speechless horror as airliners now piloted by devout believers, who were doing violence to others and to their own faith, guided airliners into those buildings, confident that they were demonstrating their deep and uncompromising devotion to Allah. Peering through the fence that guarded the rubble, we could not hold back the tears. Words lost all their power. I felt empty inside. Ordinary people, innocents, mothers and fathers, children and grandchildren, were lost with the breaking of a new day. I could only think of the songs that would never be sung, the stories that would never be told, the laughter that would never be heard, the dreams that would never come true.

The thousands who died that day were men and women of faith—Muslims, Christians, Jews, Buddhists. The shock of inhumanity and tragedy brought down in the name of faith caused me to wonder, standing there staring into that jagged void, whether believing was really worth it. I do not know whether human beings, actual people with names and faces and families and histories, can rescue religion from the mighty grips of fear and fury to become once again a voice of hope and a beacon of light in the world. The stakes are high. The conflicts are crippling us. We need to stumble our way toward a new sanctuary of talking and listening and being silent until a better word or a higher way descends upon us as people of diverse faiths.

The response of earnest believers may be simply to turn a blind eye, that is, to pretend other religions do not exist. Or, we may become louder and firmer, even abrasive and hostile, in our own religious affirmations. We have all witnessed the ugliness of religion run amok. Still, most of us have learned to be reasonably tolerant of people of other faiths, yet we usually have little interest in understanding their beliefs or exploring how another life of faith may differ or strengthen our own.

My conviction is that no person and no religion can or should presume to lay exclusive claim to God. The God of all our gods is not to be possessed. The ultimate God of the universe, by whatever name God may be called, and the personal God, which we as Christians claim to know through the person of Jesus or which our Jewish forebearers may know through the readings of the Torah, transcends all our religious traditions. Our religions offer, at best, clouded images of God. Sadly, these clouded images, springing from our religiocentric interpretations of God, have turned out to become the seedbed of religious hatred and much of the world's violence.

Like my other books addressing religious faith, this book is very personal as I try to square my own faith with the enormous contradictions that are tearing at the seams of human religion today. For that reason, I am writing, not with a scholar's pen, but with a believer's pen. As a Christian, I am writing chiefly to my fellow Christian believers. My aim is to come to grips personally and to help others come to grips with the rampant exclusivity of our diverse religious convictions.

We seem eager to believe that God is only on our side. Scholars know better. Theologians know better. Most preachers know better. It is ordinary believers who are left to twist in the gale winds of religious conflict. The people who populate our churches and mosques and synagogues do not begin their religious journeys of faith with hatefulness and hostility toward followers of other faiths. They have to be taught to be exclusive and mean-spirited. And I believe it is congregations of believers from across the spectrum of faiths who will have to save religion from the grasp of those whose goal is to use religion and the devotion of its followers to advance religious hostilities often in the cause of political ascendancy.

You and I and all our human companions from other races and ethnic groups are not abstractions and we do not come from theoretical places. We are flesh and blood, composing history on a rather inconsequential planet orbiting a small star in a galaxy adrift among thousands of others. Therefore, the future of religion is not a theological problem; it is a human problem. The very future of humankind is about nurturing new stories that will help us meet one another in a new spirit.

Admittedly, when speaking about my own faith experience, I always feel a bit awkward. It seems rather like passing around family photographs when you invite friends over for dinner. Yet, in all candor, God speaks to me not only through the Bible and Sunday homilies and the music of worship, but through questions that arise in the deep of night and through very human relationships that continue to linger in their influence within me, relationships some of which are Christian and some of which are with people devoted to other faiths. For a long while, back beyond college days, I have had this gnawing sense that there is more to this idea of God than anybody's religion can ever tell us. I suspect that no person's religion is large enough to contain God.

I have come later to believe that many other people also suffer from a growing uncertainty that their religious talk turns out to be just talk. At an early age generally, we learn the language of faith in all of our religious traditions—at least for those of us who grew up steeped in a religious tradition. We learn to communicate with the right words and to recite the affirmations of faith even before we learn what the words or the affirmations mean. However, our religious rhetoric seems, at times, to be largely severed from the "rough and tumble" of where we actually make a living and disconnected from a world in which people kill in order to demonstrate their religious devotion. If religion is more than a language to learn or beliefs to recite and becomes, instead, a prism through which we begin to see our presence in the world, we should at least learn more about the prisms through which others are looking at themselves and their world. Looking through the prisms through which others see the light of God, we too may see the light anew. We may meet God in some unexpected places.

I present these reflections in three distinct parts: Breaking Down Barriers, Touching the Faces of God, and Building Bridges.

First, I am trying to address candidly some of the encumbrances that are making it difficult to reach across our religious boundaries. Our fears and our authoritarian religious systems are shrinking us.

Second, I am aiming to open the windows of our own faith to the faith of others. Listening and learning of the faith of others may hurt our eyes, but it will not harm our spirits. All the religions of the world face enormous challenges and there is so much bad religion in the world that we often cannot see the light because it has been eclipsed by our human abuse of religious faith. While I aim to visit and touch the faces of God that are revealed in diverse faiths, I seek also to be candid about the challenges we face and the problems we must solve.

Finally, I offer a beginning, only a beginning, for building bridges that can connect peoples of faith. Our differences matter. But the people who embrace those differences matter even more.

We need, more than ever before, to develop creative communities of conversation. Conversation does not begin with talking. It begins with listening. Like Quakers of old, we need to gather in humility and honesty to face the meanness and evil which religion itself has sometimes heaped upon mankind. We should open ourselves to new spectrums of light that may emanate from faiths foreign to our own. Our high calling is to commit ourselves to building a better pathway for creating understanding and mutual respect among people of faith throughout the world.

We are yet in the adolescence of human civilization and human religion. Perhaps we will be able to conceive, through our conversations, the outlines of the larger and more transformative reformation in which we can take another great leap in our creative emergence from the primeval chaos.

PART I

Breaking Down Barriers

1

Meeting God in Unexpected Places

We should not confuse meeting God with practicing religion—any religion. Churches and mosques and synagogues are the venues where we expect to meet God or, at least, find comfort for our hurt and hope for the dawning of a better day. In truth, however, religion ranges from being central to being peripheral in our lives. Our understanding of God is often informed more by history and tradition than by personal experience. We presume God to be a Christian because we are Christian as Muslims presume Allah to be Muslim because they are Muslim. We create God in the image of our beliefs. God does not create our beliefs. Our beliefs create God.

Our challenge as believers is to reach behind our religious systems in which the nature of God is prescribed. Our challenge is to open ourselves—our minds and our spirits—to meet God as the reality that actually informs our self-understanding and the understanding of the world about us.

You and I and all the people before us have met God in unexpected places. After all, Muhammad was not expecting to meet God in Mecca. Moses was certainly not expecting to meet God in that craggy terrain scorched by the desert sun. And the people of Nazareth were clearly not expecting to meet God in an unemployed carpenter's son. It is no wonder that the light of God often slips by us. God has a habit of showing up in unexpected places.

My own most profound and life-altering experiences of God rarely came to me through the practice of religion. That practice began so early that I cannot remember not going to church. Our practice of religion is actually quite good at instructing us in what to believe and how to behave. Our ordinary lives, however, turn out to be far less orderly. If we are to meet a God that actually changes the priorities of our lives, it will have to be in the context of a world in which we are frequently confused and where good behavior struggles to overcome our inclinations to misbehave. We are more likely to meet God in our tattered-and-torn ordinary places with their broken shutters and rusted pipes than in the most high holy of holies. God lives on the street, on the subway, even inside the barbed-wire fence of Guantanomo. God has never been a captive of our sanctuaries.

As a young boy, I spent every summer with my grandparents who lived on a farm in North Alabama. The village was Hackleburg. My father had been killed in a tragic accident only a few months after I had been conceived. For my mother, it was, no doubt, a pregnancy filled with enormous grief over a terrible and unexpected loss and anxiety about how she, with two sons and a third yet to be born, would cope with a world turned suddenly upside down.

Social safety nets in 1935 were largely nonexistent. A person either had to find the courage and the fortitude—it requires both—to reconstruct some semblance of order or wander away into a fog of irresponsibility. Somehow, my mother made her way down the higher road. When my father was killed, she had $2,000. She found a way to provide for three sons and when she died at age 93, she still had that $2,000.

After I was born, my mother went to work in the school lunchroom. Neighbors and older brothers and a dog named Buddy cared for this young lad called Kirby. When World War II began to rage, lunchroom duty was replaced with work at the shipyards and then she was rewarded with the job of "Rosy the Riveter" turning sheet metal into B-25 bombers in that "steel city" known as Birmingham.

Working eight to ten or twelve hours every day, the summer months presented special challenges to this young mother. So, each summer, I would board a giant steam engine of a train headed north with instructions to the conductor to "put this boy off in Hackleburg." Summer at the farm turned out to be a magnificent fate.

That's where I first met God. Oh, from the time I was a baby, we found our way to church every Sunday. But it hadn't occurred to me in my early religious goings and comings that I might actually meet God. I also went to church when I got to Hackleburg, but I don't remember meeting God there either. I met God on the farm.

Every person, literally every person, has epiphanies that change their lives. But epiphanies are rarely dramatic events that, like a bolt of lightening, change the course of our lives. More often, I suspect, experiences are realized in retrospect as we look back toward relationships and experiences that altered our understanding of ourselves and our worlds. Epiphanies are often better recognized in hindsight.

For me, I met God in the person and the presence and the grace of my grandmother, Janie, and in the fields and the gardens where she and her husband, Peter, labored and where my earliest sense of the sacred came to life in the earth and the living things that were always full of surprises.

I watched the planting of corn and cotton, and the caring for cattle and horses, the colts and calves. I watched and shared in the nurturing of gardens, the growing of the year's vegetable store and the caring for fruit trees whose branches were bent low with peaches and apples and pears. It is hard to be present in such a nurturing, renewing environment without sensing the wonder of the world and sensing some common threads that connect our being with the earth's being.

Frankly, I didn't think much about God, but the wonder of new creations still going on was everywhere around me. The surging creative interaction of people and earth colored my soul's awareness of itself. The bearing of fruit and the surprise of digging new potatoes and discovering the yield of the earth underneath taught me little about a debatable doctrine of a remote God. Yet, the mystery of creativity and all things new in my world revealed to me that something "big" was going on in the world. It did not matter to me whether God was a Christian and meeting God at church was an afterthought.

Looking back, I suspect it is closer to the truth to say that I met God in the strawberry patch. I met God among hens hovering protectively over their brood, in the braying of the mares, and the summer storms. I met God in the cotton fields bursting out in white glory and the corn sprouting their golden tassels beckoning the harvest.

Amidst this avalanche of life and abundant mystery and incessant creativity, there was also this woman, my grandmother, named Janie. Janie was a church-going woman, but church-going, as central and regular as it might have been, did not define her for me. During the summer, she and I would walk to church along dirt roads from the farm place. After we were comfortably ensconced in the sanctuary with its ceiling fans and stained-glass windows raised part way to cajole a summer breeze, I joined her and other farmers and a few well-to-do town dwellers in the lustful singing of old-timey hymns. Then we sat back for a rip-roaring explosion of rhetoric called a sermon. I learned there that Baptists love to sing and a strong dose of fear-and-trembling religion seemed to make people feel better. I suspected that those who were there found the churchgoing and the mild trouncing they took from the preacher were penance enough for the week.

I tagged along, of course, in the churchgoing—didn't have any choice in the matter, actually. But, in all candor, the presence of Janie had a lot more influence on me than the presence of Janie in Hackleburg Baptist Church. Janie was a remarkable woman with a presence that made every room she entered a good place to be. So, long before an understanding of Jesus came along for me, I met God up close in the ways of this woman named Janie. Perhaps that is why it has never been difficult for me to think of God as a woman.

Janie was not pious in a showy sort of way. She might better be described as a farmhand, cooking big meals, darning overalls, and "putting up" butter beans and purple-hulled peas for the winter. Sitting on the front porch while the summer rain loosened the grip of the day's heat, shelling butter beans and peas, Janie told me stories of her family's migration by wagon to become homesteaders on the northern slopes of Alabama. I could sense the delight in her voice as she described running alongside the wagon in the excitement of discovering new places and new faces. Surely such a move to a new and unknown territory must have been daunting, but her stories were always filled with feelings of anticipation and expectation, of new beginnings and fresh discoveries. Joy, more than fear, dominated her storytelling and her life. She recounted to me stories about my father, Spearman. I learned of his eagerness to learn, his gentle demeanor, his inquisitive spirit, and his kindness. As Spearman walked to the schoolhouse with his little sister, Lorene, he would pick her up and carry her across puddles of rain and mud—a kindness that must have been genetic. Story after story taught me about the spirit of this woman named Janie, even as she engaged in the hard and demanding work of farm life with grace and resolve.

Her ways taught me about life and they taught me about God. She was not angry. I always felt that my mother was a little angry for being abandoned by my father who died without asking permission. Well, Janie had not exactly lived an idyllic life herself. She outlived three husbands, my grandfather, Harvie Godsey, and my stepgrandfathers, Henry Barnette and Peter Scott. Peter was the only one I knew. He was quiet, stern, not too taken with children—didn't matter. Children were not too taken with him either. Not so with Janie.

Janie embraced life and the people in her life with abandon, loving people intemperately, whether they deserved to be loved or not. The grace with which she lived was uncomplicated and even appeared at times to be unintentional, at least in a conscious, deliberate, prescriptive way.

Janie did not ever seem to be living out some external mandate to behave thoughtfully or considerately or kindly. She seemed to live from the inside out. Living from the inside out has little to do with what you say. It is larger. It has to do with your way of being present in the world. For me, Janie Dyer Godsey Barnette Scott was the earliest and clearest clue to the meaning of God's presence in the world. Her presence and grace taught me that revelations, epiphanies if you will, are not about the otherness of the divine. Revelations are about the humanness of the divine and the divinity that is locked within our humanness.

From my own episodes of meeting God, I have unyielding confidence in the power of grace to change the world. In my own experience, I learned the power of grace first through a simple but devout woman named Janie. As I grew older, my awareness of the creativity and the redemptiveness of grace was mediated through the church and scriptures and the presence and life of the person we call Jesus.

Religion, it turns out, is rarely the first light of grace. At its highest, the practice of religion is a celebration of the fact that, above all else, we are children of grace. Every world religion, in one fashion or another, is reminding its faithful that we did not get here on our own. The chief human folly, the hubris, that defeats us is pretending that we can make it on our own. If we listen with our inner ears, we surely are likely to meet God in some unexpected places.

My reflection on whether God is a Christian is driven by the conviction that many people in human history have encountered this ineffable presence of the Holy and have framed that encounter in many languages. Perhaps we can become less prescriptive about how an individual can meet God. God has many images and many names. We should remember that the human species is yet in its infancy.

Writing of other faiths, as a Christian, can never do justice either to the depth or the richness of the experiences from which other faiths spring. So, I do not write as one who is truly conversant with another faith as a genuine believer would be. My writing affirms the essential goodness of other faiths while acknowledging that all faiths are human. All of our religions fail us. Even so, by offering a brief sense of other faiths and the roots from which they sprang, I want to encourage us to be less defensive and to create an opening for knowing God more fully and hearing, even in the foreign languages of faith, the voice of God more clearly. If we have the courage to become more open, we are likely to meet God in some unexpected places. But first, we have to be honest about the barriers that are keeping us apart as believers and keeping us from a more profound experience of God.

2

The Plague of Certainty

Human religions, including Christianity, have a habit of
   trying to bring God down to size. We find ourselves
seeking to contain God within a specific religious tradition
and to tame an otherwise elusive God with catacombs of
doctrine and theological systems. As a consequence, the
profound, inexplicable, and inexhaustible experience of the
Holy that bubbles up within us like a natural artesian well
can be capped and shut off by an edgy defensiveness
regarding our conflicting religious traditions. We wind up
making God conform to our own small images. As Christian believers, we baptize God and make God out to be one
of us. It should not be surprising that believers in other
faiths do the same. Our exclusiveness, our indifference, and
our periodic hostility toward persons of other faiths is a
testimony, I believe, that we have lost our way. Religious
fervor can become the enemy of spiritual maturity.

I grew up in the Deep South steeped in an intense
religious culture. As children, we were nudged and, at
times, outright instructed to be wary of other people in the
same town who engaged in different religious practices. In
some cases, they appeared to be worshipping statues of God
in ornate and mysterious-looking places. For a lad who
attended church in a simple white clapboard house at my

grandparents' farm and a plain red brick veneer building in the city, the sight of a great cathedral with its sculpted steeples and religious chieftains dressed in black and white costumes reinforced my uneasiness. These stern-looking men and women, who seemed to have their necks held upright by stiff collars and who wore long black dresses corded with beads, were downright daunting to a young lad. So, we crossed over to the other side of the street. The distance made us feel safe.

Only later, of course, did I learn that the difference between the little white frame church and the towering cathedral was the residue of a sixteenth-century religious explosion that was born to curb the excesses of an organized church. In the aftermath, the rebels of the Reformation began to choke on their own excesses of doctrine and division. Looking back, in which case things are usually clearer, we were virtually taught to be suspicious of other Christians. Jews and Muslims were not even in the game. They gave allegiance to foreign gods and their only hope was to repent of their ways and turn to Jesus. Any thought that we should hear them out or respect their affirmations of faith never entered our minds. They were wrong. We were right. Our prejudice became the fertile soil for inadvertently nurturing bad religion. Candidly, most of us grew up with some hybrid of good and bad religion.

Fear has been the chief culprit in turning good religion into bad. In a world where the evil distortions of religious belief are casting dark shadows over the very future of human civilization, it is becoming increasingly critical that we come together as serious and devout believers to work together to bring sanity and civility to the consideration of our differing religious traditions. We cannot continue to cross over and walk blindly on the other side of the street.

In actuality, religion, as practiced today, is often more a human creation than a representation of divine intervention into human affairs. Our challenge is not only to become more thoughtful about our own religious traditions, but to act with greater respect and less indifference toward those who believe deeply in traditions that are far different from our own.

While Christianity remains the majority tradition in America and within the Western world, I believe it is appropriate for Christians to ponder whether "God is a Christian" and even be willing to listen to others who chart the course of their religious lives according to a different road map. We have to let go of our religious certainty long enough to find the courage to entertain strangers. If we do, like Abraham, we may actually dine with an angel of God. Too much of the world of faith is being tragically defined by religious arrogance. The political influence and the harsh rhetoric of people who represent narrow-minded, exclusivist, and myopic religious viewpoints have never been greater.

In this twenty-first century, the future of the Muslim world, the future of the Jewish world, and the future of the Christian world are inextricably interdependent. Even a brush with history will teach us that the Jewish, Muslim, and Christian religions are different branches of the same tree. They were born of the same soil among kindred people and, even though their history has been one marked by episodic warfare and hatred, they have sprung from common roots. Down deep, they share the same religious DNA.

As children of the West and the Middle East, we are far more removed culturally and historically from Far Eastern religious traditions. In general, the Far Eastern religions are more focused on the enlightened soul and the spiritual journey of each individual. Eastern traditions are more reflective, seeking enlightenment and a new birth. The great Western and Middle Eastern religions are more focused on the journey of faith as a community journey. We are likely to discover along the way, however, that the Far Eastern world of religion also intersects with our own religious longings.

The world of faith, like the world of economics and politics, can no longer be lived in isolation. The world of faith needs something akin to a regular meeting of the "G8" of major religious powers in order to try to reverse the spiraling course of destruction being spawned by religions run aground. What if they met not to discuss theology or whose view of God is best, but to discuss the impact for good and ill that our religions are having on the world? Each of the world's major religions has, in certain aspects, established itself as a hierarchy of religious certainty. Each tries to explain its legitimacy in the world, in part, by the claim to provide the preferred access to God. Religion becomes a world of competing revelations.

While I will focus principally on the triumvirate of faiths that had their origins in the Middle East, the conversations among these major religions of the West can themselves become myopic and exclusive. Unless we also begin serious and substantive conversations across the boundaries of East and West, we are likely to become increasingly alienated from one another with destructive consequences for human civilization. The Far East will play a prominent and increasingly powerful role in economics, politics, and religion.

Two factors in our human experience make it difficult to open a creative dialogue with other religions. One is fear. The other is arrogance. In our fear, our cloistered religious trappings make us feel safe. We come to believe that our security relies upon the expectation that we alone are fully embraced by God or that we are, at least, God's favorites. We feel safer if the world is populated by folk who look and talk and behave and believe as we do. Fear breeds the rejection of other faiths.

Arrogance, on the other hand, is based on that false sense of certainty that we alone have received the truth. That conviction breeds condescension toward less-enlightened persons. If, however, we scratch the surface of certainty, it will likely reveal an inner sanctum of teeming uncertainty.

On a human landscape that has been radically altered by the rise of terrorism, we find ourselves living in the frantic grips of uncertainty. From nuclear tests in North Korea and Iran to mindless beheadings in Baghdad and Pakistan, uncertainty reigns.

Our nation and much of the world is divided and troubled. In all candor, the security, the safety, the certainty of the American way has been an illusion for generations. This illusion was shattered by nineteen men with box cutters who put our nation in a tailspin of anger and self-doubt. Our response has been a display of power. Even so, here at the height of American power, we would be wise to look out from our lofty places and see the signs of inner decay that can erode the American spirit. The balance of human power, the balance of economic and moral leadership, may be shifting.

And in these shifting human sands, the priority, the superiority, and the self-righteous certainty of the Christian religion is beginning to crumble under the weight of its internal conflicts and its own self-indulgent disputes. We should become more, not less, uncertain of our old ways of doing religion.

The world no longer trusts Christians to be Christian. The world has watched us confuse our Christian rhetoric with the preservation of our Western culture and the sanctification of capitalist greed. At other times, it appears that we have allowed the Christian religion to become captive to a horde of Bible-worshipping, chorus-singing, homophobic, fundamentalist bullies who have alliterated answers for all of life's deepest ills. In both cases, good religion is being hijacked by egocentric arrogance.

Ministers and priests in the Christian tradition have been conditioned to think that they are supposed to ride in with the right answers wherever trouble exists. They have been trained to think their job is to rub the salve of certainty on the wounds of uncertainty. After all, they are God's priests. They understand God. They know God's way. They know what Jesus would do.

I call it the plague of certainty. In our religious fervor, we find ourselves claiming to be certain about God, certain about theology, certain about heaven and hell, certain about homosexuality. We are certain that Muslims are wrong, certain that war is holy, certain that God is a Christian. Our certainty is mostly pretense. We are doing nothing more than whistling in our religious darkness.

I believe that we will confess our faith with greater integrity if we can find the courage to confess our uncertainty. Flannery O'Connor was right when she said, "Don't expect faith to clear things up for you. It is trust, not certainty."

Our ability to raise with integrity the question of whether God is a Christian depends upon our willingness to bracket our own human commitments, even about faith, and to be genuinely open to hearing a voice that may indeed come from God and offer light we have never seen. I believe that it is possible, and even likely, that all of the major religions can become sources of light and truth if we have the courage to listen.

Faith is among humankind's greatest gifts to the progress of civilization and can also be one of the gravest threats. We should begin to explore the origins of religions in order to understand more fully the roots of our own faith and to find the common ground that is surely there.

Openly considering other faiths, their history, and their theology does not need to become a threat to our own religious devotion. We all see with limited sight, "through a glass darkly."

Our own humanness and our own spiritual understanding will be enriched by learning to listen and by affirming others as we search for common ground in a troubled world.

I grew up within the Baptist tradition of the Christian faith. My own experience has brought me to the view that the many sectarian and denominational divides within all of the major religions, including my own, bear greater witness to history, to sociology, and to psychology than to theology. These divisions are largely distractions, while becoming a source of considerable conflict in the world of faith.

None of us sees with absolute clarity. Our differing expressions of belief reflect our own personal histories and our different journeys of belief.

In November 1996, I recall being hauled before a convention of Baptist believers, about 3,000 strong. They were adamant and angry and certain that I was an unbelieving infidel because I had written in plain English in a recently published book that the Bible was indeed not inerrant, that we should not be worshipping Jesus, and that I believed that ultimately all persons are embraced by God, among other doctrinal transgressions.

With great fanfare in a hall filled with heated rhetoric, they offered a resolution to condemn and censure me for my speaking and writing about my views. The vote was not close. It was 2,000 to 1,000 to censure me and my writing as an unfaithful and immoral interpreter of the Christian faith. The experience was somewhat painful, but also strangely irrelevant. On that same day, my son-in-law, Dave Jansen, died. Twenty-nine years old. Brain tumor. The call from my daughter, Stephanie, as I left that hall of heated and hostile rhetoric, was far more important and a far greater challenge than the avalanche of vitriolic tirades. The crisis of life and faith turned angry words of convention-goers into meaningless semantics and left those words lying cold on the floor amidst the litter of programs and tracts on how to be saved. On occasions the practice of our religion causes us to lose touch with the intersection of believing and living. That intersection, more than the catacombs of our religious doctrines or the hot debates, is where meeting God matters.

Our beliefs provide us with a place to stand. While I encourage each of us to find a place to stand, we should not become so rigid or defensive that we conclude that every person needs to stand where we stand. They cannot because they have walked a different path. We can call out to one another from our differing perspectives and places, and we can learn from one another's experience. The time has come, indeed it is long past, I believe, to realize that we can learn and enrich our lives of faith not only from within the boundaries of Christianity but by listening to voices from beyond those boundaries.

The highway to a strong, resilient faith runs through the valley of uncertainty. Uncertainty can be an asset. Uncertainty and doubt can indeed become the growing edge of our faith. We do not live with perfect sight. We do not know in advance every twist or turn that our journeys will take. Christians and Muslims and Jews all live in the creases of uncertainty. The winds of doubt blow through the orbits of every person's belief. As Christians, we can go along chanting such clichés as "The Bible says it. I believe it. That settles it." In some deep night, however, our masks of certainty are likely to fall off. We find ourselves wondering and feeling guilty for wondering. We feel guilty for doubting.

In truth, the devotees of all of the world's religions need to let go of the plague of certainty. We are not people of certainty; we are people of faith. Strong faith is not born of denying wonder and doubt. Belligerent and dangerous faith is born of denying wonder and doubt. We will be more faithful Christians or faithful Jews by facing squarely into the genuine questions that bubble up within us and facing into the difficult and even tragic circumstances that invade our lives and cause us to wonder about the validity of our faith. Certainty is an illusion. Faith is not about pretending the questions do not exist. Good faith embraces uncertainty as one of the conditions of living and believing. Doubt will surely teach us that we should not believe some things.

Uncertainty can become the crucible in which we learn to listen and learn from one another. Uncertainty may be the intersection where we meet God more genuinely. As Christians and Muslims and Jews, we should begin conversations across the boundaries of faith, in part because life is not clear and precise. We do not have all of the answers and we are still refining our questions. Honest doubt and thoughtful skepticism can help to save us from the trivialization of all of our religions.

Commitment, more than certainty, should focus our living. Our faiths will be strengthened if we loose ourselves from the binding grip of pretentious certainty and find the courage to begin to listen to one another with caring and authenticity. Doing so will deepen our faith, help us achieve greater human understanding and lead us toward having a better chance of building a peaceable world.

3

The Peril of Exclusivity

The plague of certainty leads to the peril of exclusivity. Compulsive exclusivity has especially been a problem for Christianity and Islam as they are practiced in the world today, although not so true of Judaism or Eastern religions. Adherents of both Islam and Christianity seem to be racing headlong toward an uncertain future, trying desperately to demonstrate to the world, perhaps to God, surely to themselves, that their religious confession is the only true confession.

Christians need to get over it. Jesus is not God's only word. That reality need not diminish for Christians that Jesus is the Word that has set them free. Creation itself is also God's word. Adam is God's word. Mother Teresa, Muhammad, Pope John XXIII, Mahatma Gandhi, Albert Schweitzer, Martin Buber, Billy Graham, Martin Luther King, Jr. are surely words from God. Every person is a word from God that has never before been spoken and will never be spoken again in exactly the same way. The clarity and the purity of God's word spoken in each of us can become so twisted and distorted that God's real presence, which is God's word incarnated in our lives, becomes unrecognizable. God's word in us becomes obscured by the debris of our fractured existence. We cannot hear it. We do not want to hear it. Our ears become deafened to God's voice within. But God's image and God's creative presence are surely there within us, even if covered over and buried beneath our indulgent distractions by the pleasures of the "garden."

Muslims also need to get over it. The Qur'an may be God's clearest word for those who profess Islam and kneel toward Mecca five times each day and who faithfully celebrate Ramadan in the ninth month of the Islamic year. But claiming what, for us, may be God's clearest word to be God's only word is far more than human capacity justifies. It is a form of myopic self-centeredness that presumes to place ourselves—our vision and our understanding—at the center of God's universe. Exclusionary religion turns religion itself into a pagan idol.

Moreover, the notion that the Christian faith or the Muslim faith exists as a preemptive pathway to God or that the religions of Christianity or Islam provide the sole means whereby God communicates to earth's humanity or to any other forms of intelligent life that may exist in the vastness of the universe is both absurd and immoral. There is no standing place to which we can climb to assert how or to whom God will speak.

By absurdity, I mean that this idea of exclusivity simply defies reason, though I am quite aware that its irrationality may bolster its appeal in some quarters. While God transcends all our human reasoning and cannot be contained by the canons of logic, the mind is indeed one of God's most profound gifts and we need not eschew its limited power in an effort to demonstrate our devotion to God. Irrationality and absurdity carry no intrinsic value. It may be wise not to trust reason's appeal as the sole arbiter of truth. Neither should we embrace nonsense as truth simply because it seems to prop up our allegiance to certain religious doctrines. No rational pathway can lead us to the conclusion that Christians

Is God a Christian?

alone or Muslims alone have sole access to the ultimate reality that underlies the meaning of the universe.

The notion that our religion is a preemptive pathway to God may be regarded as immoral because it turns our faith into a self-centered, narcissistic religious system that says to the rest of the world that they must become like us if they wish to be accepted by God. Such arrogance is unbecoming of Christians or the devotees of any other religion. This narcissism erodes the integrity of our affirmations of faith.

We Christians should know that this kind of self-centered "if you are not with us, you are against us" thinking actually seems to be precisely the sort of religious thinking that Jesus was trying to get people beyond. As the Christian religion has unfolded into a more elaborate and sophisticated form of faith, the structures of faith have become increasingly rigid and doctrinaire. We have substituted belief in a religious system for probing the meaning and purpose of our being here. In so doing, any religion, including Christianity, can become a barrier to personal spiritual development.

Jesus' life and work, for those who came within the range of his voice or the reach of his touch, enabled people to see beyond their physical circumstances, both for the wealthy who were preoccupied with their barns of plenty and the poor or sick who were consumed by the ravages of poverty or disease. To this entire spectrum of persons, Jesus taught and lived out a way of seeing the ultimate meaning of our being here in a new light. Jesus showed us that we really come alive only when we see beyond ourselves to our essential connectedness to one another, including Muslims and Jews and Buddhists and others. Jesus called upon us to wake up to our inner connection with God, to the kingdom of God within. Our being here, the being and presence of another person, and the presence of God are all irrevocably intertwined.

Jesus taught and lived among his disciples the transforming truth that if they were to know God, they would have to be prepared to meet other people in a new way. Islam also began as a way of enabling believing Arabs to see one another in a new way. In both cases, their followers were taught that our ultimate well-being is tied intimately to the well-being of others. Most of our faiths essentially teach us that to wish ill toward others or to act destructively diminishes our own character and blinds us to the presence of God.

In practical terms, relating in a new way seems to mean looking out for people we may not even like, binding the wounds of people we may not know and listening to somebody who believes in her heart that nobody understands. The call to meet other people in a new way does not stop at the boundaries of our faith. If we are to be Christian, we must bind the wounds of Muslims and Jews just as surely as we should bind the wounds of other Christians. The way of grace knows no geographic or religious or ethnic boundaries. Muslims constitute about one percent of the population of the United States. If we Christians treat them with disrespect and harsh rhetoric or defile their sacred texts or desecrate their sacred places, our actions become a testament that we do not believe or accept the new way of living and relating, embodied for us in the life and the presence and the words of Jesus.

Meeting people in a new way can be tough business. It was tough business as I grew up as a young professional in the heat of the civil rights era in the 1960s in America. It was tough business for Muhammad in the 600s. It is tough business in the twenty-first century when fires of terror have been unleashed and are raging wildly across our world.

In the 1960s, my wife Joan had the temerity to use her talent in music to teach young black children in the racial cauldron of

Marion, Alabama. The simple act of a white woman teaching black children unleashed ostracism in a small Southern town. Meeting people in a new way is tough business. It is tough business in America where we must chart a new way for dealing with illegal immigrants. Neither walls nor amnesty are likely to be a sufficient answer. It is tough business dealing with abortion and the sanctity of life. It is tough business in addressing the issues of homosexuality and gay marriage. Social and political conflicts are tough business. Territorial conflicts are tough business. Conflicts are tough business in Gaza and Jerusalem, in Tehran and Beijing.

While our human conflicts can be daunting, we Christians have to come to grips with the reality that there is not much that appears exclusive about the mind or the actions of Christ. Beggars, lepers, adulterers, and Samaritans were all welcome. Jesus broadened the circle of God's embrace. Insofar as the Christian religion has come to offer itself as the exclusive bag of answers to life's most difficult questions or a proprietary window through which the light of God shines on the human race, Christianity has simply become one more world religion competing for center stage, while sorting through its own episodes of darkness. This myopia is Christianity's greatest challenge and its most insidious weakness.

Rejecting exclusivity does not require abandoning the central place of faith in our lives and rejecting exclusivity does not require abandoning our commitments. Being a Christian, I confess that my understanding of God and my sense of what it means to be here at all have been informed and shaped by the presence, the words, and the actions of Jesus. Without question, Jesus plays a powerful and enduring role in understanding my life and my relationships. So, I confess my faith and invite others to experience the light by which I live. And while I am grateful for the light which comes to me through the presence of Jesus, I clearly am not fully enlightened or somehow magically devoid of shadows, of uncertainties, of valleys of distress and distrust and misunderstanding. Our understanding is broken. Our vision is blurred. That reality should foster within us a larger measure of tolerance and openness.

If we are to offer the light by which we live as something worthy to be considered by others, we should also have the courage to consider the light by which they live. It is possible that some persons who do not call themselves Christian and whose own lives are shaped and guided by a different light than our own have achieved a level of spiritual maturity and have come, by other means altogether, into closer harmony with God than we. None of us is fully enlightened. We do not see the way with perfect clarity. At best, we are simply pilgrims along the way, confessing the light that illumines our soul and we should be open to embracing others who live by another light. Otherwise, we are closing off echoes of the voice of God.

In our own faith as Christians we have so far to go. We are only in the infancy of believing. Christians are not, at this moment, even able to embrace one another. The Pope of the Roman Catholic Church, who is generally regarded by the non-Christian world as being the chief priest of the Christian faith, is roundly rejected by great hordes of the Christian church as having any relevance to Christianity. In the rural South of the 1950s where I grew up, anti-Catholicism was alive and well. Some Christians rejected Catholics as being close kin to pagans. Now, I realize there was enough paganism to go around. The Christian church is tragically and irrevocably divided and has been for centuries. This radical division only darkens the light that is able to break through the vestiges of Christianity.

Our best response, however, is likely not to create some new monolithic Christian organization. That should not be attempted, principally because it cannot be done and any efforts to overcome these breaches would only generate a new brand of sectarianism.

We are, after all, human. The splintering of the Christian church, as with the splintering of other religious traditions, is simply a testament to our frail humanity. The Christian church, while initially being inspired by the life and presence of Jesus, was developed as a human institution. It is subject to all of the limitations and characteristics of human organizations. Personalities, priorities, and historic periods condition its emergence. Our religions become blinded by our own egos. The Christian church is no different; the Muslim faith is no different.

A more achievable goal is to take these divisions within the church less seriously, realizing that they are probably more sociological and emotional than theological. Christians belong to a common community of faith. In this respect, of course, Christianity is not unlike any other established religion in the world. Since we are not as familiar with them, we may think of Islam or Buddhism as integrated religious traditions. As we look closer, of course, we find that these religious traditions are also plagued with broken expressions of their traditions. All religion is human religion.

In Christianity, the failure to overcome our fractious condition makes it even more difficult to address the challenge of our exclusivity. Many Christians actually believe, having been taught by priests and preachers, that in order to be Christian, one must accept the exclusiveness of the Christian way. It goes like this: By Christ and Christ alone can one be saved, citing the words of Jesus: "I am the way, the truth, and the life. No person comes to the Father except by me." It is indeed the case that, for an individual for whom Jesus Christ is the light of the world, Jesus is the pathway through which God's presence and nature have been brought down to earth. It is simply unnecessary and it is clearly saying more than we know to claim that the light by which another lives and calls by a different name is a different light and an inauthentic word from God.

Living faithfully and nurturing the inner life of the Spirit does not require that we know that Muslims and Hindus are doomed to some godless abyss unless they come over to see the world and God through our "looking glass." The person of Christ is a gift to be celebrated, not a tradition to impose. We do not enrich our own faith by declaring the invalidity of another's belief.

For Christians, the light of Christ is surely transformative. It changes everything. All of life, every relationship, including one's self-understanding, are transformed by the life and teaching of Jesus. The wonder of the Christian faith, however, is in no way related to the validity or invalidity of another's belief. When we reflect more seriously on how we should regard the religious commitments of others, it seems reckless to assume that God the Almighty of the universe, may have spoken in only one language. To be sure, we can be confident that the one God of the universe speaks with one voice. It is certainly reasonable to assume that other persons have seen authentic and genuine light from God. I need not judge the worth of the light that guides their lives.

For me, the light that has come to me through the total presence of Jesus has changed the way I see myself, the way I see the world and the way I see God. Insofar as that light is embodied in a limited and frail way in my life, it becomes a witness to the light of Jesus Christ. But to be sure, I have observed what seems to me to be the light of God in the lives of others who do not claim to be followers of Jesus. I think of Sri Ramakrishna; I think of Martin Buber; I think of Mahatma Gandhi; I think of the Dalai Lama; I think of Moses and Abraham. It is not for me to say whether the light that informed their lives is or was inauthentic or spurious. The better course is to listen and to learn from them, to embrace them as children of God, to love them without condition and to treat them as equals before God.

Recovering from our compulsive exclusivity means recognizing that, above all else, grace and light come from God. Neither we nor any of our religious companions on the human journey are made acceptable to God by anything we do or anything we believe. God embraces and God enlightens. The bedrock of the life of the spirit is not that we believe in God but that God believes in us. God believed in Muhammad. God believed in Siddhartha Gautama. God may use many instruments to come to us.

Sometimes God comes to us in spite of our religion. The nurturing of the human spirit occurs as we open ourselves to know our own inner lives more intimately and more genuinely. We nurture the spirit by listening in quiet solitude, learning from the language of Jesus, and listening to the language of others who see a different light, and relating to one another as unique reflections of God's image. Every person is a gift to the world. The most redemptive way to connect with others is to see the face of God in each person we meet.

As we recover from our proclivity to be exclusive and arrogant, we can begin a new journey of learning and growing in our spiritual lives. We also create the foundation for beginning a new level of respectful and affirming conversation with persons who are devoted to other beliefs. Those conversations can become the pathway that leads us beyond the peril of exclusivity.

4

The Tragedy of Fundamentalism

Virtually all of the world's major religions today, to some degree, have become victims of rampant and uncompromising fundamentalism. Furthermore, the rise of fundamentalism has become the chief culprit causing the transformation of some of the religions of the world into instruments of war rather than instruments of peace. The tragedy of fundamentalism causes a devout but twisted young man to blow himself up in a crowded marketplace in Jerusalem, or to become a bomber in Olympic Park, or to kill a medical doctor in Kansas. Christian fundamentalism and Muslim fundamentalism, in particular, are making it more difficult to open avenues of conversation with other world faiths. But, all fundamentalism whether Jewish or Christian or Muslim is woven from the same fabric. It is born of the same religious instincts and its consequences are all too often tragically evil.

The error of fundamentalism springs chiefly from its inordinate claim to possess absolute truth. Every religious faith, of course, makes certain truth claims generally based upon a revelation mediated through scripture or prophets or even institutions such as the church. These claims of truth often determine the traditions and the practices of our faith and serve as primary reference points for understanding and interpreting our faith to others. The difficulties arise when our claim to know the truth is translated into religious or theological assertions that we believe have absolute validity. Believers, then, are required to give unqualified assent to their "truth" or they are deemed to be unfaithful.

For a decade, I watched Baptists in the South feud and fight, spewing out enraged rhetoric, quarreling and maligning one another in order to conquer the giant corporate enterprise called the Southern Baptist Convention—the largest corporate religious prize in America. The Bible was the focus of those vicious quarrels. In preachments, the fundamentalist takeover was about rescuing Baptists from the heresy of the infidels who they believed were "soft" on inerrancy. In reality, it was and always is about power. The church's riches were at stake. The inerrancy of the Bible echoed across the hinterlands as the compelling wedge through which a small band of fundamentalists conquered the religious hierarchy called Southern Baptists. It was an awesome display of power politics, laced with impressive strategy and full of deceit and treachery. Ostensibly, it was a fight about the Bible. It bears repeating, however, that at its heart fundamentalism was and always is about power and control.

The claims to accept the Bible literally and to regard the Bible as inerrant seem unsustainable on the face of it. People do not punish their children by death as commanded in Deuteronomy. Many passages in the Bible are inconsistent, even contradictory, and the descriptions of Jesus and the events of Jesus' life differ substantially among the four gospels. The notion that the Bible is infallible and inerrant will unfortunately appear to be nothing more than blind bigotry, used by fundamentalists to curb the inclination of believers to think for themselves. Thoughtful Christians should not be intimidated into believing that their faithfulness as

Christians is somehow related to their willingness to affirm the inerrant truth of holy scripture.

The notions of inerrancy and infallibility are treacherous human fallacies. People do not always hear God aright. To ascribe infallibility to the Bible is wrong, and it is wrong for the Qur'an as well. It is simply one more misguided and frail effort to possess God. For Christians and Muslims, inerrancy takes books that are pivotal and central to our faith and turns them into objects of worship. When we Christians do so, we are forced to accept descriptions of God's will that are woefully incompatible with the God we have come to know through Jesus. I do not believe that God actually ordered Joshua to kill every man and woman and child during his invasion of Canaan. I do not believe that God orders the stoning of women or children or gays. We have to weigh scripture against the word that we have heard and seen from God in Jesus.

According to Jesus, not every word of the Bible is created equal. Quoting scripture, Jesus said, "You have heard that it was said, 'An eye for an eye and a tooth for a tooth.' But I say to you, do not resist the evil person." For Jesus, those words of scripture missed the mark of God's word. When asked about the greatest commandment, Jesus did not reply that all 613 of them were equally important. Rather, he said, "Love the Lord your God with all your heart and with all our soul, and with all your mind. This is the first and greatest commandment." And in a similar exchange, Jesus said of the great commandment, "Do this and you shall live."

We should not be blinded by our human yearning for a certainty that gives rise to our idolatry of the Bible. The Bible is complete; revelation is not. Revelation is the end of the Bible but the Bible is not the end of revelation. God's light has not gone out. God has not fallen silent. We should study the Bible and learn and be inspired through its words, while we follow Jesus and worship God, who continues to speak to us. We need to break through the paralysis of inerrancy and break down the idolatry of biblical infallibility which have been spread over us by fundamentalism like a tent of darkness. It is far easier to take the Bible literally than it is to take the Bible seriously.

Fundamentalism in Christianity represents, I believe, an abuse of Christianity and a radical distortion of Jesus' life and message and even his death and resurrection. Fundamentalism also represents an abuse of Islam and an abuse of Judaism. In all these cases, fundamentalism arises from the same instincts within humanity to create clear authority in a world that is uncertain and to foster morality in a world that is immoral.

Within Christianity, this abuse is nowhere more evident than in the fundamentalist doctrine of "substitutionary atonement," one of the five pillars of Christian fundamentalism. While the cross in Christianity has become a powerful and profoundly important symbol of our faith, it has also been misused as the critical focus of faith and the foundation of the meaning of salvation. This doctrine has become so pervasive that it has seeped into the mainstream of the Christian interpretation of salvation and, on any given Sunday, may be heard from the pulpits of earnest ministers across our land. It is a telling example of how a convoluted explanation of Jesus' death becomes a doctrine that Christians are taught to believe in order to explain their urgently desired claim "to be saved." Simple, unfettered grace is just too good to be true. Therefore, we feel obliged to create an elaborate justification for God's grace. The doctrine affirms that our wrongdoing warrants an ultimate and eternal punishment by God and Jesus steps in as our "substitute."

I grew up in a religious culture where the notion of substitutionary atonement was not a theory. It had the full status of absolute truth. Preachers learned it. They preached it. Congregants were expected to believe it. After all, it makes sense in a culture that operates on the reasonable expectation that all of us have to "pay our dues."

When I grew up in the rural South, late summer was always revival time. Revivals were mostly built around the idea of substitutionary atonement. The local preacher would invite another preacher, usually a friend, sometimes a circuit-riding evangelist, to hold a revival meeting. The meeting lasted at least one week, sometimes two. On the farm, revival time always came after the crops were "laid by." It was the lull between the intense work of "chopping cotton" and "plowing corn" and the eager time of waiting for the harvest. This late summer lull before the harvest was a great time to make a renewed commitment to the faith. Farmers needed all the help they could get to secure a good harvest.

The nights were hot. The regular churchgoers and those not so regular felt obliged to show up for revival preaching. As people gathered, the singing began lifting the rafters with revival hymns—"The Old Rugged Cross," "Almost Persuaded"—so familiar, people could sing them by heart. The men were slow to drift in from standing outside, chewing tobacco and comparing the state of their crops. The singing was a way of warming up the congregation before the main event.

Revival sermons were usually a preacher's best. As a visiting oracle, he could deliver the finest specimens of his homiletical repertoire. Visiting evangelists were showmen. They had a small but well-honed package of sermons that were choreographed to have a compelling impact on all who listened. Some such sermons became legendary, such as "Payday Someday" by the Reverend R. G. Lee from Memphis, Tennessee. Good evangelists could set the town buzzing about the revival meeting.

There was a formula for successful revivals. The vigorous singing and the passionate praying—prayers themselves that could make their hearers begin to weep—were meant to raise the emotional intensity of the revival gathering. When the preaching began, the congregations settled in for a concentrated dose of "fire and brimstone" rhetoric.

Good preachers caused people to lose all track of time. Powerfully, the preacher summoned with startling realism the load of guilt that rested comfortably in the inner recesses of the listener's consciousness. His goal was to bring sinners to an overwhelming sense of "conviction," causing the heart and soul to palpitate with a frightful awareness of personal sin and guilt. Effective preachers would paint vivid pictures of the waiting torment. He would remind us that if we died that night on the way home without "accepting Jesus," we would suffer in hell for eternity. Even as a young lad, I found these colorful and passionate images to be far-fetched. I cannot say that I didn't find them frightening. Yet, an angry God sending people off to an everlasting and infinite hell because of some stupid, finite sins didn't seem right. Even as a young child, that was not the kind of God I wanted to believe in.

At these revival meetings, there was, of course, enough sin and guilt to go around. When that sense of utter depravity became intense and overpowering, the preacher offered a way out. When the vivid fires of hell began to sear into people's comfortable world, they became afraid that they were going to burn forever because of those secret sins that they had hidden away. By then, the evangelist was ready to close the sale. Just as they began to feel the fire, he proclaimed, "Jesus died for you. Come to the foot of the cross, where all your guilt can be washed away. Jesus paid it all." By this time, substitutionary atonement was a welcomed relief from the heavy burden of fear and guilt. Sweaty regret was overpowering.

People didn't come to revival meetings to hear that God loved them. They came to revivals to be saved and to be told in passionate and compelling language what they already knew— that they were not worth loving. They were wicked and headed straight for a fiery hell whether the crops come in or not. But there was a way out. The penalties of sin had to be levied. The sinner could escape his dreadful fate if and only if he accepted Jesus as his "substitute." Substitutionary atonement was his only hope.

This message of substitutionary atonement, of course, winds up making God responsible for Jesus' death. We make God out to be a God who has to get even. The books must be balanced. The debt must be paid—sounds a lot like the way we do business. It makes God in our image.

We can admire the cross, be inspired by it, or build theories of salvation around it. Jesus did not die to appease an angry God. Atonement is not about appeasement. The death of Jesus becomes atoning only when it becomes a power within our own lives. Jesus was calling his disciples and us not to admire the cross but to embody the cross. We have to participate in the life of the cross. There lies the important meaning of being "crucified with Christ." Living the salvation life means seeing and living our being here in our own specific world in a new way. It is not about following Jesus abstractly or verbally; it is about engaging our lives in a new way.

In reality, we Christians need to learn that Jesus' presence in the world was not about doing something that would enable God to love sinners and to forgive them. If we can set aside these theological explanations, the truth of the Christian faith is likely more simple and direct. In flesh and blood, Jesus embodied God's unconditional love and forgiveness in our kind of world. The word "unconditional" seems so hard to hear. The gospel is not a transaction to make; it is a gift to receive. God loves us and forgives us already—no conditions, no prerequisite, no plans of salvation to follow. Sheer grace. Grace is a difficult word for fundamentalists to hear. While well-intended, whether Christian or Muslim or Jewish, fundamentalists are inclined to substitute fear for grace.

As a result, one of the principal failures of fundamentalism, and evangelists who use fundamentalism as a tool of their rhetorical trade, is that it turns a religion of forgiveness and life into a religion of fear and death. Neither Christianity nor other religions should permit themselves to become used and abused as religions of fear. That transformation is inevitably a sign of decay. Fear and suffering are the very evils from which people need to be delivered. Using fear in the service of converting people to faith contradicts the faith that we wish that person to embrace. The fundamentalist notion of an eternal hell has the outcome of transforming Christianity and Islam into religions of fear. The heart of the Christian faith and the Muslim faith is not about fear. Faith is never about fear. Throughout the world, people are drowning in fear. Fear, either in your religion or mine, will never generate hope or peace.

Neither the Christian religion, nor the Muslim religion, nor the Jewish religion, nor the Hindu religion represents the hope of the world. We are all ultimately children of grace. Grace means that our hope does not rest in the affirmation that we believe in God. Our hope rests in the reality that God believes in us. God believes in us more than God believes in our religions. God's unconditional embrace transcends all of our religious systems. God's love is the antecedent of, not the consequence of, our following Jesus or our faithfulness to Allah or to Yahweh.

If we take seriously that we are all children of grace, we should acknowledge that even if we believe that fundamentalism is an egregious mistake, fundamentalist believers are not themselves evil or bad people. They may be frightened people, but they are also God's people. Fundamentalism may make them feel safer. But, let us be clear. Good people who become victims of fundamentalism are fighting for the reliability of their faith. They are looking for an anchor in the midst of life's tortuous waters. Consequently, they sometimes embrace a human and flawed religion as absolute truth and as a hedge against life's difficulties. Human religion—Christian, Muslim, Jewish, Hindu, and others—is always flawed. None of us possesses perfect insight nor do we have a right to claim an unfettered vision of God. Whatever else human religion reflects, it surely reflects our humanity with all of the shadows that characterize that humanity.

In our humanity, we long for the security of doctrines and dogma. Doctrines are simply the residue of religious experience. Doctrines—Christian, Jewish, or Islamic—are efforts on the part of earnest believers to convey the power of relating to God through the eyes of their religious experience. Because language is weak and inadequate, we reach for other means to convey the power and the mystery of our experience of God through story and metaphor, through music and poetry. But we should recognize that all our efforts to communicate our experience of the holy whether through doctrine or metaphor, will be tentative and flawed, always subject to the limitations of human language and human communication.

Judaism, Christianity, and Islam alike are not about what we say; they are about who we are and what we do. Each of these faiths has to do with changing the center of gravity of our lives, not simply changing the content of our language. In Islam, bowing five times a day while facing Mecca and praying devoutly is about changing the center of gravity of our lives.

The Jewish faith guides its followers toward living in covenant with God, the one relationship that defines every other relationship and every action of one's life. It, too, changes life's center of gravity. The Torah teaches and instructs. The act of holiness does not lie only in reading the Torah, but allowing its reading to become a forum for God to speak to us. The real test of whether the Torah serves as an instrument for connecting the believer and God is whether a person's way of being in the world is changed by hearing the word from God. Fundamentalist Judaism identifies human language as the word of God and requires assent by the believer in order to be a faithful Jew. The covenant with God, a living bond which language can only poorly describe, is replaced by a large structure of belief, made with fallible human hands.

Islamic fundamentalism suffers from a similar set of challenges. Muslims, whether Shia or Sunni, have, in some cases, raised their human interpretations of the Qur'an to a level of absolute truth. Muhammad would, no doubt, be appalled by the divisions within Islam. Fundamentalist Muslims are seriously distorting the meaning of Islam and, like Jews and Christians, are using their religion for political purposes. In their highest expressions, Christianity, Judaism, and Islam center their beliefs and their practice of faith on compassion and peace.

Clearly, some Muslim clerics and believers are using their Islamic faith as a justification for wanton human destruction. Their use of this fundamentalist distortion is reinforced by self-serving promises that, by believing these distortions of faith and offering their lives as martyrs, they will have immediate access to holy immortality.

This fundamentalist twisting of the Islamic faith is hardly more than religious brainwashing. It veers markedly away from the deepest and greatest traditions of Islam. It is a manifestation of religion gone bad, using people who may be young and poorly educated, or who, in other cases, may live under distressed financial or political conditions, to carry out the political agenda of those who wish for Islam to gain world ascendancy. The leaders themselves may be well educated and even wealthy, carefully using the sacred writings to justify their actions. It requires a narrow and distorted reading of the Qur'an to find foundations for the violence and treachery of Islamic fundamentalists. Fundamentalism is certainly contrary to the larger message of the Qur'an, contrary to the spirit and life of Muhammad, and contrary to the meaning of Islam. Indeed, the term "Islam" is based upon the Arabic root word meaning "peace."

But lest Christians be too harsh in their judgments of the twisting of the meaning of "jihad" into a holy war against the West, the Crusades in the thirteenth century were similar in purpose and scope to fundamentalist Islam. In the Middle Ages, Christians were arguably even more militant than Muslims. Today's weapons are far more destructive than they were in the Middle Ages, but the instincts that give rise to terrorist acts by Christians, Muslims, and Jews are essentially the same.

When we examine the roots of fundamentalism, we find several themes in common. In the first place, fundamentalism is a form of religious devotion turned in on itself. Instead of trusting God, fundamentalists trust their religion. Their goal is to establish the superiority of their position, religious or political, by gaining ascendancy and defeating their challengers. Fundamentalists, Christian and Muslim alike, are in a war to win the world. Jews in Palestine are in a war to establish the integrity of their "holy land." The only way to be sure that we are God's favored people is to defeat those who believe otherwise. In doing so, we destroy those who are infidels, thereby demonstrating that we are favored by God. Religious faith falls victim to the demonic desire to control. It was the same desire that captured Adam and Eve's heart in the Garden.

Fundamentalism places the individual rather than God at the center of belief. It is a self-serving, myopic brand of belief and reinforces self-centeredness as the key to achieving hope and success.

Religious success is built on believing the right things, eliminating all hints of doubt and, thereby, being assured of God's acceptance and an ultimate reward of "going to heaven." Fundamentalism is nothing less than religious idolatry. It is one more golden calf at the altar of which adherents achieve religious success.

Religious success becomes very much akin to secular success and often becomes a surrogate for people who have not achieved "worldly" success. Yet, some others have achieved every measure of worldly success and are attracted to a religious system that offers clear answers and doubt-free doctrines. For fundamentalists of every stripe, winning is everything. In Christian circles, winning is measured by the metrics of monies raised, church attendance, and souls saved. Bigger is definitely better and the growth in people and money are the primary evidences of God's favor. Religious engagement is all about winning the religious sweepstakes.

In fundamentalist Islam, winning has also come to mean victory over the West. The killing of infidels is the holy work of the army of Allah. In fundamentalist Zionist Judaism, winning is establishing the state of Israel as the land of God's promise and defeating all of those who challenge the rights of the Jewish homeland.

One of the common themes of religious fundamentalism has been its use of the world of politics as a forum for extending its power and influence. This use of fundamentalism as a platform for political control was nowhere more evident than in the takeover of the Iranian government by Islamic fundamentalists under the leadership of the Ayatollah Khomeini. Civil government was overthrown in favor of a theocratic government. Religious law was substituted for civil law as the ultimate authority.

Christian fundamentalists have tried, often successfully, to exercise power in American democracy through such initiatives as Jerry Falwell's "moral majority" and Pat Robertson's *700 Club*. The goal of these institutions is to influence elections and to place into high political offices individuals that are sympathetic with the rigid religious doctrine of Christian fundamentalists and to constitute themselves as a voting block.

The dangers of this political fundamentalism, whether Christian or Islam, are self-evident. In effect, fundamentalists are arguing persuasively to their adherents that political actions and decisions should be governed by God's will. Such an affirmation even seems unassailable to devout believers. The difficulty, of course, arises with interpreting God's will. Neither the Bible nor the Qur'an provides specific guidance on the politics of America or the Middle East. Consequently, the "will of God" turns out to be an interpretation of some individual or group of believers who seeks to impose their vision of God's will on the larger civil society. The earnestness of these interpreters, notwithstanding, they are themselves human interpreters whose own history and prejudices affect and often determine their view of God's will. In effect, they substitute their will for God's will and use the language of faithfulness to God to enforce compliance with their specific political agenda.

The emergence of fundamentalism in both Western and Middle Eastern culture and society no doubt results, in part, from the genuine moral decay and rampant secularity of the contemporary world. In the face of what appear to be declining moral standards and the threats to the traditional roles of religious institutions in managing behavior, the fundamentalists seek to reassert the priority of more puritan behavior. They use the power of guilt and the fear of eternal rejection by God as a means of motivating more allegiance to traditional moral prescriptions and religious practices.

Fundamentalism focuses far more on personal morality than social morality and, even in the political arena, the main focus of fundamentalism is on personal moral choices. Fundamentalists are typically more silent when it comes to social morality—issues of racism, or poverty, or sexual discrimination, or issues such as capital punishment or war. Strangely enough, the Bible and the Qur'an, the sacred scriptures that fundamentalists revere so highly, are far more outspoken about poverty and reaching out to the marginalized and to those who are sick or imprisoned or poor. While the fundamentalists may seek political gain through a vigilant defense of high personal moral standards, they often do not become a force for addressing the larger moral issues that plague human civilization. Substituting political prominence and influence for becoming a more vigilant voice for overcoming violence and for lifting up the weak and the oppressed remains one of the defining tragedies of fundamentalism.

Fundamentalism in every religion represents our most resilient and pernicious barrier to creating authentic conversations among peoples of faith. Each religion claims that it offers the sole means whereby God's word may be heard. When we adopt that point of view, any measure, from ruthless evangelism to the wanton killing of infidels, can be rationalized as saving people from a fiery hell or destroying the enemies of God. The rise of fundamentalism and its periodic resurgence, for example, in America or in Iran, always sets the stage for the abuse of faith. Good religion turns bad. Good and thoughtful people are driven away from the fountains of faith because of the evident evil of religion itself.

If we are ever to build bridges, we will have to find the courage within our circles of faith to reject fundamentalist religion as a fearful and destructive force. Fundamentalist Islam, fundamentalist Judaism, and, yes, fundamentalist Christianity represent religion that has gone astray, bringing more darkness than light. Fundamentalism is more the embodiment of human sin than God's salvation.

PART II

Touching the Faces of God

5

The Language of God

The metaphor of "touching the faces of God" can serve us well only if we are prepared to broaden dramatically our use of God-language. We need not be frightened to hold our language up to the light. Much of our God-language comes from mythology, especially Greek and Sumerian mythology which were resources for Judaism, Christianity, and Islam. Indeed, when we speak of God, we have no choice but to resort to myth and poetry, to parable and stories. God is not a fact to be discovered in our laboratories. God is truth to be experienced in our history. When I speak of touching the faces of God, I am not speaking of elaborating a factual description or delineating different doctrines of God. People are touched by God before they call God's name. They hear God's voice before they speak of God's presence.

While the notion and the language of a personal God are profoundly important to us as Christians, the notion of a personal God was not as important to Confucius, Lao Tze, or the Buddha. For them, as for Christians, however, the ultimate reality to which we all belong and before which we all fall silent, language failing us, can make us a new creation. In matters of faith, including the Christian faith, a carefully constructed doctrine of God is not the *sine qua non* of religious reality. Our religious reality is that compelling passion, that centering force, what theologian Paul Tillich referred to as that "ultimate concern," that defines and transforms and gives meaning to our human experience.

Christianity, Islam, and Judaism are all defined by a radical monotheism, and while these differing religions call God by different names, it may reasonably be argued that they are acknowledging the same God. In Far Eastern religions, the idea of God refers more to the ultimate "way" or the "eternal order" within the universe, which also resides within each individual. While connecting with the reality of God in very different ways, religions in both the East and the West are arguably searching to find the same ultimate meaning of the world and deliverance from suffering and evil. Their God-language, however, is radically different.

The theological constructions of the idea of God emerge in all of our religions as largely human creations, reflecting both human insight and human blindness. Our differing cultures, indeed, give many faces to God. This diversity in our human understanding of God does not simply reflect the gods of different religions. It reflects different images of God within the same religion, including Christianity. In the Old Testament, God is Creator, Destroyer, Judge, Redeemer, Deliverer, to name only a few. In the New Testament, God is Father, Counselor, Forgiver, Teacher, to mention a few. God wears many faces.

In every religion, the transforming religious experience is turned into a religious system. Its complex and esoteric language sometimes turns out to be a barrier to actually knowing God. Doctrines of God represent the rationalization of our human experiences of God. Dogma intellectualizes God's presence in the world and interprets God's presence and intervention in history. In considering Christian doctrine, and religious doctrine generally, the idea of God as an intellectual concept becomes, at times, the greater preoccupation than God's actual presence in human affairs. In religious doctrine, our views of God can become formulaic and sterile, a kind of ideological creation. For this reason, before we look at the gods of our religious systems, I propose to look briefly at the genesis of our human experience of God.

Describing our experience of God is likely to be more akin to an artistic rendering than a rational definition. Words so often fail us. Every world religion resorts to literary descriptions because literalistic descriptions of God turn out to be hollow and cold, devoid of passion. I am among those believers who do not believe that there is an external thing "out there" in the universe that properly bears the name God. God is not a noun. God is not a substance in the world to be located rationally or apprehended doctrinally. In their most insightful moments, I believe that none of our major religions rests its faith on the existence of "a" God somewhere in the universe.

The existence of a God is clearly not the focus or the preoccupation of Far Eastern religions. Paul Tillich was right, in a sense, to say, "God does not exist." His affirmation was not meant to deny the reality of God, but to warn us against imposing our human structures of time and space on the reality of God. God lies behind space and time and the existence of our universe. Even when we use the word "behind," we are using a spatial metaphor. My point is that space and time and existence have a beginning and an end. The beginnings and the ends of existence occur within the eternal presence of God. Language betrays us. For that reason, God is often more accessible through art and imagination than through science and analysis.

Many of the more important components of our human experience are not accessible through intellectual analysis. Loving someone is not the result of an intellectual analysis. Joy is not always the outcome of an intellectual analysis. We should not disregard the profoundly significant role of the human mind in understanding the world and also understanding each of our world faiths, but it will require more. Understanding the human experience of God will not only require lucid and rational thought. It will also require the understanding of the poet and the insight of a psalmist. Speaking God-language is not a way of laying claim on God, of getting God in our grasp so that we can settle the issue of God once and for all. It is more about trying to discern episodes of God's presence in human experience without respect for whether those who experience God are Christian, Muslim, Jew, or Hindu.

The word "God" holds a large reservoir of meanings. One person's God is not necessarily the God of another. In our own personal histories as well, the God of one era is not always the God of another. From time to time, we find ourselves desperately trying to hold onto gods in which we no longer believe. Much of our lives are spent in search of a God we can trust. Our gods change. I remember as a college student reading the little book by J. B. Phillips, entitled *Your God Is Too Small*. That small volume intersected my life at a strategic moment, helping me claim the freedom to let go of gods in which I no longer believed. A part of growing up as believers has to be learning to let go of gods in which we no longer believe. The Old Testament presents pictures of God which for many of us are no longer persuasive. Not believing some of those images does not mean that the Bible is not true; it means that the Bible is not always factual. No one story of God's presence discloses God fully: lesser revelation should be judged in the light of higher revelation.

Changing gods, of course, can be a scary experience, sometimes accompanied by guilt for leaving the gods of our childhood. We may learn what we do *not* believe before we learn what we *do* believe. We may find ourselves wandering through a period that

Is God a Christian?

feels like a sacred emptiness. Individuals may change their religious identity radically because they discover, through new light, a higher and more noble understanding of God. Our language of God changes.

Believing intensely is always filled with passion and risk. Few things can be more powerful in our lives than believing in someone or something. Believing carries the power of commitment, even when we can see only vaguely and our understanding is clouded. Believing is filled with risk because in choosing to believe, we are also choosing to disbelieve. Tragically, the passion with which we disbelieve in the God in which others believe sometimes becomes the test of whether someone really believes in the "true" God.

Becoming more mature as sojourners of faith enables us to understand that believing in God is not ultimately about denying the reality of other visions of God. A person's particular and specific vision of God should not be regarded as the only possible or reasonable vision of God. The God above all our limited perceptions of God always lies beyond our grasp. God is not to be possessed and the gods that we claim along our spiritual pilgrimage remain only imperfect images of God. The journey of belief lasts a lifetime. We have to keep growing, keep learning, keep gaining new insight.

As we grow and change, sometimes more maturely, perhaps more immaturely, our gods change. When we change gods, it is called conversion. If we want to know the name of our God, it may turn out not to be the God of our religious language. Our language may be contradicted by our living. The actual God of our lives and our personal histories may have little to do with the God of our religious affiliations and our language. Sunday after Sunday, millions of us recite:

I believe in God the Father Almighty, Maker of heaven and earth.

And in Jesus Christ his only Son our Lord; who was conceived by the Holy Ghost, born of the Virgin Mary, suffered under Pontius Pilate, was crucified, dead, and buried; he descended into hell; the third day he rose again from the dead; he ascended into heaven, and sitteth on the right hand of God the Father Almighty; from thence he shall come to judge the quick and the dead.

I believe in the Holy Ghost; the holy catholic Church; the communion of saints; the forgiveness of sins; the resurrection of the body; and the life everlasting. Amen. (Apostles' Creed)

But we may wonder quietly whether the God of our creeds serves as the integrating clue to our lives. It does not matter much what we call God. The God we serve is that reality, that person, that conviction, that passion, that moves and centers, that orders and energizes us.

The issue is not likely whether we have "purpose-driven" lives. We all have purpose-driven lives. The issue is the character and content of that purpose. The fact is that we serve many masters, many purposes. We may be worshipping monotheists while we are practicing polytheists. It is commonplace that we find ourselves having to be many people, wearing different and even conflicting faces, consumed by competing priorities, chasing after many gods. Many of us, perhaps most, live without a single, vital, integrating center. We are possessed by the moment and by the master who has gained ascendancy for the time. We live fractured lives, following many masters, trying to be true to many voices, living out many purposes.

The call of faith—the Christian faith, the Muslim faith, the Jewish faith, the call of the Buddhist way—does not come to people who do not believe in God. The call of faith comes inevitably to people who believe in many gods. The landscape of faith is not that we believe too little. We believe too much. We are vulnerable to the call of the moment. Being without a center, we are left to worship many gods, to join every parade, to follow every new banner.

If we are to find the genesis of our experience of God, we must be prepared to acknowledge that the God we actually worship and around which we organize and center our lives is often far from the God we confess with our lips. The most important journey of religious experience is to bring the God we proclaim and the God about which we center our lives into greater harmony.

Human beings have a long history of creating gods. Wherever societies have emerged, insofar as we are able to document and chronicle the unfolding of human history, we can locate the struggle to identify some reality that is not subject to the fragile life we experience, a reality that can sustain us and can bring order and meaning into our lives. Earliest humankind identified with unseen spiritual forces that they believed to be present in all of life, even inanimate life, such as rocks and trees. People wanted to touch this reality, to communicate with this reality, and as they personalized that reality, their gods took on anthropomorphic forms. Gods were created in the image of people. From Zeus to Yahweh, God has been made in our image.

The question about God is a peculiarly human question. Only the human species appears to raise the question of God. There is a mystery about human life, and about our own being here that inevitably gives rise to the language of God. The issues we call religious—man, woman, life, death, eternity—are born of the human spirit. No mere fragment of clay would raise such issues. They reside within us. Our questions break out like sweat on a marathon runner. While human life is experienced as fragile and transitory, we human beings long for a world of immortal beings, or at least, we want to achieve some sense that the brief span between life and death does not tell the whole story of our lives.

I describe this intersection by saying that you and I live between the "not yet" and the "no longer." Clearly, there was a time when we were "not yet" here and it appears that there will be a time when we will "no longer" be here. Does living between the "not yet" and the "no longer" define us or is there some transcendent dimension to our being here? Through myth and epic poetry, civilizations created elaborate religious symbolism to convey their hope that their being here has significance that will endure. In a world of change and loss, we wonder whether there is something that endures.

So, the idea of God is born amidst this universal human awareness of frailty and mortality. The history of human civilization, at every turn, reflects this human struggle to connect with a more enduring reality, to know some reality that transcends the boundaries of human birth and death.

The earliest peoples were not principally concerned with proving the existence of God. The question of God's existence is an American question, a European question, not so much a question of the Middle East or the Far East. Such questions belong more to rational and scientific inquiry. In the world of religion, the notion of God did not come into being as the conclusion of an argument or a logical deduction. Thomas Aquinas, perhaps the greatest and most influential Christian theologian of all times, offered a series of rational "proofs" for the existence of God, taking his clue from the philosopher Aristotle. But the God whose existence Aquinas was seeking to demonstrate is a God already known to him through worship and faith.

Our God-language was born as a means of making sense of our being here. The notion of the divine, whether achieved through reason, revelation, or both, becomes a means of shaping a foundation for how we ought to behave, how we ought to relate to one another, and for understanding what our world is all about. Making sense of life gives rise to our yearning to experience God. Either life is a futile survival from birth to death or our being here is animated with higher purpose and with spiritual significance. Relating to the Greek gods or to the Hebrew God became an avenue for finding meaning beyond the fleeting frame of time and space. Relating to Allah became a means of finding cohesion and moral purpose among wandering Bedouin tribes.

The creation of the notion of a sacred world where gods and goddesses experience enduring life is a critical part of human history. Divine beings are believed to be stronger, to have greater knowledge, and even to be immortal. Humans long to participate in this higher world. That participation is chiefly through ritual and myth, through symbolic sacrifice and worship. Religion is born as a context for relating to and becoming a part of an enduring world.

Wherever we venture into religious history, we find widely divergent experiences of the struggle to encounter the divine or to experience Nirvana. Conceptions of God vary and our human language of God emerges and changes as our human perception and experience change. The idea of God in one culture or one generation may be discarded by a different or subsequent generation or culture. The encounter with the divine experienced by the Persians and the Hebrews was different, but through myth, symbol, and ritual, they were each seeking to connect with the divine, with a holy essence, that could give them meaning and a hope for immortality.

If we are to sustain belief in God, we should remember that all images and notions of God are not created equal. Not every idea of God that is born amidst the human journey and even reflected in the Bible or the Qur'an or the Torah deserves to be sustained. Throughout human history, we have experienced evidences of a spiritual reality which we convey in poetry, music, ritual, and symbol that transcends ordinary human affairs.

So, our God-language is an effort to capture the power of transcendence and to convey the belief and the hope that the universe and our fragile existence have meaning beyond the brief days that constitute our lives. Our images of God vary in every culture and, from time to time, become outmoded and ineffective. But in every stage, they bear witness to the human longing to participate in a holy and enduring essence that transcends the vulnerability of our ordinary lives. We want to be liberated from suffering and pain and death.

Creating gods is something human beings have always done. Our language of God is generated by human experience itself. Whether Jewish, Christian, or Muslim, we long to know and be known by a God who transcends and makes human experience possible and gives meaning and hope to our ordinary lives.

The question of God, then, bubbles up from deep within us. We are never content simply to be here. We want our being here to matter. We want to know how we and those before us came to be. Our own being, though fragile and terribly limited, drives us toward reaching for that reality that is not so fragile or limited. Our own "beingness," our actual being here, leads us toward the "beingness" of God. We are but we are also dreadfully aware that we could not be. We long to know and to participate in being that is not bounded by not-being. The ongoing "beingness" of God suggests that, though we can "not-be," we are here and our being here is ultimately made possible by the power and presence of God's being. We do not always know what language to use to connect to that being, but we yearn to see God's face. God's reality is that being that is not bounded by the fragileness of human existence. Our language is a frail way of saying that without God's being, nothing, including ourselves, would exist.

Our lives, which I like to think of as fiery episodes of God's being and presence, are like sparks of divine light. Because God is, we are. Each of us might be regarded as a wholly unduplicated spark of light, a packet of creative energy in this vast expanding universe that bears witness to the ultimate creative presence of God. Our being here bears witness to God's presence. Our language of God is meant to affirm our conviction that God's presence means that Reason and Light will ultimately endure. Because Light endures, that episode of light and reason that bears our individual name will never go out. We have always been and always will be a part of God's presence.

In the pages that lie ahead in this section, I am aiming to open a small window through which the light of other faiths might shine through. These pages will provide only elementary glimpses into faiths that scholars and believers have expounded in tomes of great literature. A reader's interest or curiosity may prompt him or her to explore a more thorough understanding of another faith. My goal here is different and more simple. Opening a window is meant to encourage a new openness to explore diverse faiths more seriously, to meet believers of other faiths with more gentleness and compassion, and to encourage us to let go of the fears that are keeping us from meeting and talking to one another in good faith across our religious boundaries. Our world will become a better place and we are even likely to experience God's presence more profoundly when we begin to see one another as children of one God.

6

The God of Abraham, Isaac, and Jacob

The power of story has never been more evident in any of our religions than in Judaism. From the stories of Creation, which too often are mistaken as scientific or historical accounts, to the dramatic stories of the Exodus and the Exile, the Jewish faith has endured with compelling passion and persistence because it has been a community of belief that is held together by their common experience of God's presence and intervention in their history. Only their sacred stories enable human history to make sense.

The story of Israel begins with Abraham. Historically, Abraham is the father of Judaism, Christianity, and Islam. Each of these world religions claims their beginnings in the life and pilgrimage of Abraham. The Hebrew Bible attributes the beginnings of Israel to the call of God to Abraham's family, specifically to Abraham's father Terah, to pick up his belongings, his household, and leave the city of Ur and travel toward an unknown destiny—a destiny known only to God.

Ur was a prominent Sumerian city in what is now modern Iraq. There Abraham's family, a tribe of Semitic people, had settled into the urban life of this Sumerian city. By the standards of rural and urban life 3,000–4,000 years ago, Ur was an urban landscape with large stepped temples called ziggurats, the ruins of which still exist in Iraq. Unlike the Semitic nomads, the Sumerians were more urban and settled people, sometimes credited with the invention of writing and mathematics, the calendar, and sophisticated construction. Since Abraham's family was more nomadic in background, it would not be surprising that Terah left Ur and set out toward a new land. They traveled north along the Euphrates River to the place called Haran in modern-day Eastern Turkey. Haran was clearly only a stage in their travels, but it was here that Terah, Abraham's father, died.

While the first eleven chapters of Genesis are composed of stories of creation and human frailty, the writings beginning with the story of Abraham's family seem to be cast in the form of a rudimentary history enriched with myth and legend to record the roots of Jewish tradition. Abraham is described as having settled in Haran and, following the death of his father, Terah, God spoke again to Abraham. Clearly, Haran was never intended to become a final destination. The journey to Haran was a journey on the way to the land of Canaan. Nevertheless, Abraham's forebearers had settled in Haran and apparently prospered there.

The biblical story handed down through centuries of oral tradition records God speaking to Abraham:

> Go you forth from your land, from your kindred, from your father's house to the land that I will let you see. I will make you a great nation. I will bless you and make your name great and you will be a blessing. And all the peoples of the earth will find blessing through you. (Genesis 10:1-3)

The significance of "journey" should not be underestimated in understanding the Jewish faith. The God of Abraham is a God that directs our human journeys. We do not find the will of God simply through contemplation. We meet God as we go. God calls us to make our way toward strange and uncharted places. The progress of human life and human civilization is linear. Abraham finds hope and meaning in his life not by worshipping God in a settled life, but, by faith, striking out to places unknown, responding to the voice of God. Creation is a journey. Judgment is a journey. Redemption is a journey. And every journey is a story. Creation and judgment and redemption are not simply events that belong to the past or the future. They belong to our journey in the present. For Abraham, as well as for you and me, the promised land is not a place to go; it is a journey to make.

Journeys are always an important part of the human story within the Jewish tradition—the journey to Canaan, the sojourn from Canaan to Egypt, the journey with Moses toward the promised land, the journey to and from exile. God is present in these journeys and the Jewish faith affirms that wherever they go, God is present. We build altars along the way that mark our defining experiences. Wherever God's presence confronts us or whenever God's presence captures us becomes a life-defining altar.

This notion of an ever-present God of the universe had its birth in Abraham. For that reason, the monotheistic religions of Christianity, Islam, and Judaism all view Abraham as the progenitor of their faith. Abraham is the prophetic voice that inspires the journeys of all Islamic, Jewish, and Christian believers. Each of these three great religions are confident that they are the authentic children of Abraham.

Rooted in the journey of Abraham, all of these monotheistic religions turn out to be religions of action—movement, discovery, and challenge of the unknown. Much of the Western scientific spirit and the spirit of exploration may be traced to this approach to understanding a personal and social history that was common to Judaism, Islam, and Christianity. That historical consciousness bred a culture that was lured by the unknown and the undiscovered. That consciousness formed an awareness that God, the ultimate reason of the universe, is always with us in our journeys into the unknown. Rather than a remote and detached overseer, God is actively engaged in history and the world.

As Christians, Muslims, or Jews, we wander and, while our wanderings inevitably confront the mysteries and the uncertainties of the unknown, our faiths teach us that we never wander outside the presence of God. Our understanding that all our wandering takes place as a sojourner of God is a gift from Abraham to Judaism, Christianity, and Islam.

One stunning characteristic of Judaism is the centrality of family. Family always tells a story. The significance of family to Jewish life was a gift from Abraham. The vision of God communicated through the intimacy of family was present throughout the journeys and the nation-building. Family was central throughout the prophetic warnings and the lonely exiles of the family of Israel in a strange land. Family embodies God's real presence. Jewish people, generally even today, have a deep sense of family. Family traditions serve as a cohesive touchstone of personal identity throughout life. There are no isolated individuals. One's identity and worth spring from belonging to a family.

We were recently invited to be a part of the seder meal in the celebration of Passover by my Jewish friend, Melvin Kruger. Above all else, the seder was a family gathering, including Melvin's brother Paul, Melvin's son Steve, and Shelley and Deborah and Aunt Sadie and her son Stanley, and Jack and Melvin's daughter Gail, and Elise and even the youngest child, Allison, and us, whom they embraced warmly as extended family. Together, as family, we participated in a magnificent ceremonial meal. For us, and I sensed even for them for whom it is a regular ritual, the seder meal was a moving and heartening experience. The importance and centrality of family were the centerpiece of that event, as they were for the children of Israel in Egypt. Throughout Jewish history, beginning with Abraham, family has provided comfort in grief, encouragement in hardship, and light for their journeys. The family embrace, for Judaism, is an existential incarnation of God's enduring presence with them.

Abraham's son, the one through whom the family of Israel would unfold, his only son with Sarai, was Isaac. He produced another son with Hagar whose name was Ishmael. The lineage of the Jewish descendants is traced through Isaac. The heritage of the Arab peoples is traced through Ishmael, Isaac's half-brother. This kinship became the legendary foundation for interpreting the historic conflict between the Jews and the Arabs. This conflict became intense in the twentieth century when Zionist Jews began to acquire land from the Arabs to establish the State of Israel. The view of the Jews, of course, was that the land belonged to the Jews from the time of Abraham and only the scattering (the Diaspora) of the Jewish people during the Roman domination of the first century resulted in the land being occupied by Arabs. Therefore, from the point of view of the Jews, they are simply reclaiming their birthright.

The absence of a son and the later birth of Isaac revealed Abraham as the archetypal man of faith, not in a theological sense of believing devoutly in God, but in his trust that God keeps promises. Abraham believed God when God told Abraham that his family would become a great nation, even in the face of the fact that Abraham had no children.

Later, the biblical writers tell of Sarai's giving birth to a son and because Sarai had laughed at the notion that she would, at her advanced age, bear a child, the child was named Isaac, meaning "laughter."

The measure of Abraham's faith would be stretched further. Abraham was told by God, according to the biblical story, to sacrifice his only son, Isaac. This story in which God demands that Abraham sacrifice his only son seems outrageous for our moral sensitivities. Yet, this archetypal man of faith took Isaac and climbed Mount Moriah to sacrifice Isaac in obedience to God. And as Abraham took the knife to slay his only son, without whom there would be no family or nation, God intervened and provided an alternate sacrificial lamb. Abraham's unconditional trust became the foundation for building a holy nation.

While the notion that God would demand such sacrifice might seem repulsive on the face of it, the epic story becomes a telling revelation of the centrality of trust in God. The real point of this story, morever, is not meant to demonstrate only the faith of Abraham but more clearly to demonstrate the faithfulness of God. God keeps promises.

Beyond his role in this story of Abraham's faith and God's faithfulness, Isaac was chiefly a bridge between the more interesting characters of Abraham and Jacob.

Isaac and his son, Jacob, worshipped the God of Abraham. On his way to find a wife amongst his kindred back in Haran, Jacob dreamed of meeting God who blessed him and confirmed the blessings that were given to Abraham, namely, that his descendants would be a great nation and possess the land of Canaan. And Jacob named this place where God confirmed these promises Bethel, meaning the "house of God." Jacob dwelled in Haran where he developed a family and became economically successful. But the time came for him to go back to Canaan, the land of promise, where he had deceived Isaac and cheated his brother, Esau, of the family birthright.

The story of Jacob encountering Esau on his way home underscores a dramatic transformation of Jacob's life. Jacob had to face up to the consequences of his treachery and deceit in the person of Esau. On the night before meeting Esau, Jacob separated himself from his family and belongings in an apparent act of trying to spare them from any tragedies that might flow from his date with destiny as he met his brother Esau the next day.

The night before meeting Esau became perhaps the most important night in Jacob's personal history. In the deep night, Jacob wrestled with a stranger that he believed to be God and he named the place "Peniel" which means "the face of God." This altar experience left Jacob with an enduring limp and a new name—signs of transformation. His name was changed to "Israel," meaning, "The One Who Wrestles with God." This experience changed who Jacob was and how he walked upon the earth. That humbling, life-changing event enabled him to become an instrument of God's presence. The Bible is replete with stories of how ordinary, and often flawed, individuals are used to achieve the ultimate purposes of God. The Islamic, Christian, and Jewish religions are not mostly about how God uses saints, but how God transforms unholy people into serving as instruments of the holy.

With the dawning of a new day, Jacob and Esau embrace one another as brothers. They put away their history of hurt, and the twelve children of Israel (Jacob) become the progenitors of the people of Israel.

The sojourn of the children of Israel, their slavery, and their subsequent deliverance is another pivotal story in the Jewish understanding of God. Joseph was the son of Jacob born to his favored wife, Rachel. The saga reads that because of the jealousy of Joseph's brothers and half-brothers, they, with convincing intrigue, sold Joseph into slavery and he was carried into Egypt. In that place, all of Joseph's misfortune turned to fortune. He became a slave in the household of the ruler, Potiphar, and resisting the sexual advances of Potiphar's wife, the strong and handsome young man was thrown into prison. In prison he became known as an interpreter of dreams, finally being brought to the pharaoh himself. Hearing the pharaoh's dreams, Joseph interpreted them to mean that Egypt would experience seven years of plenty to be followed by seven years of famine. The pharaoh was so impressed with Joseph that he placed him in a position of authority over the empire in order to prepare for the years of famine.

Jacob and his remaining family came to Egypt to escape famine of their own. In an intriguing account, the family was reunited as they encounter their lost and forgotten brother Joseph, and Joseph became their hope for survival in this strange land. Throughout the story of Israel, we are reminded over and over again that God is present and is transforming human failure and malice into instruments of hope and forgiveness. What people mean for ill, God transforms to be used for good purposes, the lesson being that no amount of human evil can ultimately thwart the purposes of God. In Egypt, the children grew in number, power, and influence.

The prelude to the Exodus event occurs as subsequent pharaohs became uneasy, even frightened by the burgeoning influence of the people of Israel. Oppression followed, and Israelites, once favored and powerful, became enslaved and powerless.

The story of the Egyptian abuse of the children of Israel introduces us to the second most powerful and influential figure in Jewish history, Moses. Moses was the central figure in what is the defining event for Jewish life and history—the Exodus. Through Moses, God became a personal Deliverer, the Liberator, the Savior.

When we examine the major Western and Middle Eastern faiths, Judaism, Christianity, and Islam, we discover that while they share a common history, they have distinct identities in large measure because of the focus of each faith. In Islam, God is defined by a book, the Qur'an. In Christianity, God is defined by a person, Jesus of Nazareth, and in Judaism, God is largely defined by an event, the Exodus from Egypt.

The story of Moses remains one of the most compelling epic events of Jewish history. Beyond the era of Joseph, the growing population of Israelites became a greater perceived threat to the society of Egypt. Responding to this sense of threat, the ruling pharaoh of Egypt ordered that all Jewish male babies be killed at birth. This decision seems a bit curious since children are born by the female offspring. Nevertheless, the epic story recounts the saving of Moses by his mother, who engineered the discovery of the baby Moses by the pharaoh's daughter. Moses, hidden on the shores of the Nile by his mother, was found and brought to the pharaoh's house where he was reared with his biological mother acting as a nurse for the child. Growing up in palace splendor, yet nurtured in the religious sympathies of his mother, Moses became a child of both worlds —the world of the pharaohs and the world of the oppressed Israelites. The inevitable clash of values bred by the disparate worlds erupted as Moses, seeking to address the wrongful treatment of the Israelites, slayed an Egyptian overseer. Word spread of Moses' impulsive killing of an Egyptian and Moses had no alternative but to flee for his life into the desert.

Moses settled in the rugged land of Sinai, married and became a sheepherder among his wife's family. The Moses story reached a high moment in an event that changed his life and destiny. No doubt full of remorse and a strong sense of isolation, Moses seemed content to live out his days in the wilderness of Sinai. Yet, we are confronted with this dramatic tale of Moses wandering on the back slopes of Mt. Horeb where he was startled by a flaming bush that was not consumed. As Moses drew near to observe this remarkable sight, he heard the voice of God calling to him by name, "Moses, Moses," and Moses replied, "Here I am." This calling of Moses turned out not only to be the turning point for the personal history of Moses, but the words with which the Exodus began. Moses was told that he was standing on holy ground and that the God that was calling to him was the same God who had called out to Abraham, Isaac, and Jacob. Moses was assured that God had been present, taking into account the abuse of the Israelites at the hands of the Pharaohs and that he, Moses, was to be the agent of God in delivering God's people from oppression. Moses valiantly objected to the call of God and initially, in exasperation, cried out, "Who am I to say who sent me? What is your name?"

God replies: "YHWH." [Yahweh.] God now has a name.

The Hebrew writing of Yahweh occurred without vowels and appeared to be an archaic form of the verb "to be." The translations offer endless possibilities for interpretation, including, "He causes to be," "I am that I am," "I will be what I will be," and simply "I am," being itself. God's presence and being is more like a verb than a noun. In other words, God is action and presence more than object and substance. God is more like a verb than a noun.

God, who was known to Abraham as Elohim, now has a name. Moses was able to convince the children of Israel that Yahweh was the God of their fathers—Abraham, Isaac, and Jacob. Henceforth, the God of Israel is to be YHWH, a name so holy as not even to be spoken. (To this day, "God" in English translations of Jewish literature is sometimes written as "G-d," and pronounced "Adonai," "Lord.") God has a name and, above all else, is the Redeemer, the Savior, the Deliverer of the people of Israel.

The test of wills is fierce but pharaoh was ultimately no match for Yahweh. The children of Israel were brought to safety through the Sea of Reeds, and the rising tide of the sea crushed the pursuing Egyptians. Yahweh is the faithful deliverer of his people. Now wandering about in the rugged wilderness of the Sinai, this disorganized and disoriented band of Israelites was slowly crafted into a community of believers through the leadership of Moses. That too was a long journey. It took forty years.

There in the wilderness, a covenant was established between Yahweh and Yahweh's people. The Exodus and the covenant that issues from this event shaped the history and the faith of the Jewish people and continues to shape that history even to this day. That covenant is crucial to Judaism. The covenant was described by the writer of Exodus:

> *You have seen what I did in Egypt, how I bore you on eagle's wings and brought you to me. So, therefore, if you will hearken to my voice and keep my covenant, you shall be a special treasure among all people. Indeed, all the earth is mine, but you shall be a kingdom of priests, a holy nation. (Exodus 19:4-6)*

This covenant of responsibility, more than privilege, was sealed with the Ten Commandments, which, in effect, spelled out the impact upon our daily affairs of living in covenant with God. Though the Rabbis actually count a total of 613 commandments in the Torah, the Ten capture the basic moral and spiritual principles that bear out the impact of living in covenant with Yahweh. This God of Abraham, who might have been viewed as a more local God in Canaan, was the God of the earth, an active participant in human history, guiding people and history to its highest destiny. Yahweh is the God of the pharaohs, the God of the wilderness, and the God of the Promised Land of Canaan. God never deserts us and is the ultimately faithful redeemer.

The third great interpreter of God's identity in Jewish history was King David. David was both human rascal and interpreter of the divine. David comes into our focus first as a boy, a shepherd lad, a singer of psalms who brought solace to his interminably tortured predecessor, King Saul. This young lad confronted the powerful and mighty Philistine in the legendary figure of Goliath. The simple and the innocent stood up to the high and mighty, making the point that Yahweh is greater than human might and takes the simple faith of young David and delivers the mighty and powerful Philistine into his hand.

Following Saul's rather disastrous and jealous rule, David became the King of Israel and, for the first time, the tribes of Israel were united into a cohesive nation. The capital was moved to Jerusalem and David established his authority as the great, indeed the greatest, King of Israel. David was a charismatic and visionary leader of Israel who ruled the nation with a combination of boldness and treachery.

The biblical accounts of David do not treat him as a hero saint. To the contrary, we are able to see David in all of his devilish, cunning, and deceitful ways. Both murderer and adulterer, David yet became the human vehicle through which the golden era of the Israelite state emerged and Yahweh became clearly known as the God of Israel. So David became another central figure in Jewish history through whom God's presence was made known and to which Jesus' lineage was linked.

Abraham was the prophet who became the father of both Israelites through Isaac and Arabs through Ishmael. Moses became the instrument of God in the defining event of Israel's history, the Exodus from Egypt, and the covenant which created the enduring significance of the Exodus event and David who became God's voice in shaping Israel into a nation.

At each stage of the story of Judaism, Yahweh is the integrating force of Israel's history, from the call of Abraham to the divine establishment of the united Kingdom of Israel. Though the people of Israel did not, especially in the early years, deny the existence of other gods, Yahweh was increasingly identified as the one

God of Israel. The well-being of Israel was conditioned on their serving no other gods. This devotion to one God became pervasive in the child of Judaism called Christianity and the offspring of Abraham called Islam.

The Hebrew prophets also played a prominent role in helping to enlighten the Jewish community regarding the nature and the presence of Yahweh in the world. The prophets heralded troubled times, some speaking words from God as the specter of Assyrian domination loomed on the horizon of the kingdoms of Israel in Northern Canaan and Judah in Southern Canaan. Later, other prophets spoke of the coming of the Babylonian captivity and the implications of having to practice and to sustain their faith far away from their homeland and its traditional temples. So, the understanding of Yahweh in the Jewish faith was substantially enriched by the voices of the prophets, some of which I will identify here so as to clarify the prophetic contributions to the Jewish understanding of God.

During the eighth century BC, Amos and Hosea both preached to the powers of the Northern Kingdom (Israel), providing new and compelling insight into God's nature. After the people of Israel moved into Canaan and gradually began to prosper, the monarchies began to feel self-sufficient. They carried on the semblance of faith through sacrifices and rituals, but the practice of faith was having little bearing on the conduct of life. Avarice and greed among the rulers and the priests were rampant, as was their olympian confidence that Yahweh would always protect Israel from harm.

Amos and Hosea heard and proclaimed a new and startling prophetic word. They made clear that Yahweh would not be a protection from the consequences of their immoral behavior and their empty worship. Amos offered only searing judgment and unrelenting scorn for the religious practices of Israel. Amos proclaimed that Yahweh said, "I hate and despise your feasts. I take no pleasure in your solemn festivals" (Amos 5:21-24). Instead, Amos proclaimed if you want God's blessing, "Let justice roll down like mighty waters and righteousness as a mighty stream."

Amos gave us new language and insight by warning that we cannot separate worship from behavior. If worship does not change how we treat the weak and the dispirited and how we behave, worship is in vain. Mere ritual is not enough. Furthermore, the culture of greed and disrespect for the poor reflected their growing distance from Yahweh. The prophets believed that this egocentric lifestyle would lead to their destruction and indeed it did at the hands of the Assyrians in 722 BC. Through the eyes of faith, the Assyrians became the instrument of God's judgment on empty religion.

The message of Hosea was similar to Amos. He proclaimed that Yahweh desired faithfulness and mercy, not sacrifice and burnt offerings (Hosea 6:6). In their comfort and pride, they had abandoned the inwardness of Yahweh's covenant. Again, ritual alone had no value. Ritual without inward devotion and outward beneficence was worthless.

It was the prophet Isaiah that later began to clarify for the people of Judah in the Southern Kingdom that Yahweh was not simply a God of Israel and Judah. Yahweh is the God of all peoples. Yahweh is the ruler of all the earth. The universalism of Yahweh, then, was first clarified by the prophets.

Almost 150 years later, when some of Israel's population was carried off into exile into Babylon, the prophet Jeremiah made clear that Yahweh was not a God tied to a particular place (Jeremiah 31:33, 34). God would go with them into Babylon. In addition, that exile could become an occasion for the recentering of faith and meeting Yahweh in a new way in a foreign land. This change of address could itself become an instrument for learning to worship Yahweh more authentically. They could become an instrument of Yahweh's will for his people in times yet to come. In this way, the universality of God's power and the promise that God would never abandon was reinforced by the exile in Babylon. Though they were "strangers in a strange land" that experience could awaken an awareness of God that had been lost in the comfortable environment of Canaan.

The prophets taught Israel that loneliness and suffering can become a centering force for religious devotion. The prophetic word in Jewish literature provides a warning to those who profess faith but who behave as though faith makes no difference in how we relate to others, especially the poor and broken. Worship without compassion is empty and vain. But the word of the prophets which also rang clear was that, though God warns us of the consequences of our perilous pathways of greed and self-reliant egotism, God will never abandon us. No land is so remote and no condition is so dire that God's spirit is not present. The prophets proclaimed that the time is never too late to turn one's face toward God.

The story of Judaism does not end with the prophets or the Old Testament. Rabbinic Judaism has continued to evolve, and even in the era of Jesus, the School of Hillel shared much in common with the teachings of Jesus. For example, Hillel who lived from about 60 BCE to 20 CE, is famously quoted as teaching, "What is hateful to you, do not do to your neighbor. That is the whole Torah. The rest is only commentary." As Judaism has developed through the centuries, it is clear that this historic faith has not remained frozen in history. While Judaism has suffered from the sectarian divisions that plague every world religion, Judaism continues to speak to the heart and the actions of the faithful and holds high the understanding of God as a God of mercy and compassion. The rabbis have continued to interpret and reinterpret the Torah in successive ages to make it relevant for new generations. As a result, the children of Israel continue to be called to experience the holiness and the accord with God's will that comes only by embodying Yahweh's spirit in the world.

The Jewish faith remains a particularly resilient and courageous story of human frailty and God's persistent devotion. Despite depression and hardship, despite oppression and discrimination, despite tribulation and sorrow, the people of Israel steadfastly found their cultural and religious bearings in their faithful worship of Yahweh. This same Yahweh promised never to abandon them. Because of the conviction of that promise, generations later, Judaism remains a major and a compelling voice among the religions of the world.

7

The God of Muhammad

Islam has, in certain respects, paralyzed us in America. A decade ago, we might have regarded mosques and women dressed in veils as strange or out of step with the culture, but, for the most part, would not have felt hostility or hatred. But when the religion of Islam was hijacked by a band of fundamentalist true believers who committed dreadful atrocities, we were shaken to our foundations. We have grown suspicious of Muslims generally and out of the bowels of our enormous pain and hurt, good people have found themselves seeking revenge even when it turns out to be against innocent people.

If we are to recenter our souls and regain our sense of sanity when meeting people of different faiths, if we are to overcome our justifiable bitterness and resentment, we must be prepared to seek understanding in a world that is inclined to mount hostilities because we are consumed with rage.

We discover, at the outset, that the God of Islam is close kin to the God of Abraham, Isaac, and Jacob. If we are ever to overcome the world's religious conflict, we have to begin by listening to the earnest voices arising out of other faiths. That willingness to listen is nowhere more important than with respect to Islam. We should not be content with caricatures. Understanding requires listening and learning. Our religious commitments can easily turn into religious prejudices when we describe the faiths embraced by others in ways that debase their inner and higher meaning. Of course, the actual practice of our different religions is a part of the problem. The distortions of faith created in all of our religious practices frequently bear false witness to the inner meaning of each of our faiths.

For example, as Christians, we would not like for the meaning of Christianity to be defined by the barbarism of the Crusades or by the killing and maiming which some Christians have done in the name of God, such as the "Army of God," a group of domestic terrorists in America. Similarly, our view of Islam is often shaped by the dreadful destructiveness of suicide bombers or the massacre of innocents. I believe, and most Muslims believe, that the work of the terrorists is antithetical to the true meaning of Islam.

On the other hand, the evil work of terrorists under the guise of being faithful Muslims should not be disregarded or ignored. It is a brand of Islam that has lost its way and unfortunately has brought suspicion and distrust among many people, both Christians and non-Christians, toward all Muslims. Muslims and Christians and Jews should speak out far more vigorously about the evil actions of persons claiming to be faithful followers of their religious traditions. Any religion can become demon-possessed and used for evil and inhuman purposes. Islamic terrorism is a demon-possessed distortion of Islam.

Dr. Sheikh Ali Gomaa, who presides over the Dar al Iftaa, Egypt's supreme body for interpreting Islamic law, recently wrote (*Islamization Watch*, Thur. 8 Oct. 2009):

> *We issue thousands of 'fatwas' or authoritative legal edicts—for example affirming the right of women to dignity, education, and employment, and to hold public office, and condemning violence against them. We have upheld the right of freedom of*

conscience, and the freedom of expression within the bounds of common decency. We have promoted the common ground that exists between Islam, Christianity, and Judaism. . . . As the head of one of the foremost Islamic authorities in the world, let me restate: The murder of civilians is a crime against humanity and God punishable in this life and the next.

Judaism, Christianity, and Islam each have sick and demented expressions of their religious traditions but the evil forms of religious tradition and the dark episodes of religious behavior should not be used to define or describe the rich traditions of either Judaism, Christianity, or Islam.

If we are to understand and even appreciate the contributions of Islam, we should begin by trying to understand the roots from which Islam sprang.

Islam became for the Arab people the kind of unifying force that Judaism was for the children of Israel. Muhammad (ca. 570–632 CE) was a gifted individual and, in many respects, his work enabled the Arab people to coalesce as a united people from a plethora of tribes of nomadic wanderers. Before Muhammad's critically important work, the Arab culture was hardly more than a federation of Bedouin tribes, struggling to survive and often pitting themselves against one another. Tribal violence was commonplace. These wandering tribes daily faced the possibility of extinction.

Muhammad himself was a member of the tribe of Quraysh, a group of Arabs who became very successful in trade. Their primary settlement was in Mecca. As a result, the families of Mecca became rich and powerful and in the seventh century the city of Mecca became a center for trade and finance.

In Bedouin culture, the members of each tribe developed great dependence upon one another. There was safety only within the tribe. Being highly vulnerable, the wandering tribes provided for the sustenance of the peasant and the most marginal among them. In the growing wealth of the city of Mecca, community stewardship was being replaced by a capitalistic individualism in which wealth-building and greed were becoming the prevailing values. Muhammad believed that unless the people of the tribes of Quraysh, and later all of the Arab people, could be governed by more transcendent values, such as compassion and caring, that the Arab tribes would disintegrate into a morally bankrupt culture.

The wandering tribes of Arabs were involved in endless warring and tribal conflicts. In that desperate and dysfunctional culture, Muhammad became a powerful instrument for a more united and morally sensitive culture of Arabs. By the time Muhammad died in 632 CE (or 10/11 AH, Anno Hegirae—the Islamic year) he had achieved what would have seemed impossible. Muhammad had virtually single-handedly molded the loose federation of Arab tribes into a social and political culture sustained by the devout influence of Islam and the faithful allegiance to one god, Allah.

Muhammad was not an immediate hero among his own people in Mecca or among Arabs. The odds were against him. After experiencing the intense revelations of God's speaking through him, he initially made very few converts. Slowly, more converts recognized the authenticity of these revelations from Allah. The Meccan leaders in power became increasingly alarmed by Muhammad's influence and, in part for self preservation, he migrated to Medina in 622 CE (1 AH). At the request of the people there, he became not only the prophet of Allah, but the chief political statesman of the community. He ruled in Medina with a respected combination of compassion and justice. He was able to mold this city of warring tribes into a coherent community devoted to Allah. His reputation as a statesman, as a leader, and as a prophet of Allah began to spread more broadly across Arabia. What followed was a struggle for the hearts and minds of the Arab world between the people of

Medina led by Muhammad and the nobility and the richer leaders of Mecca. Wars ensued. Eight years after Muhammad left Mecca, his armies defeated the Meccans. These former persecutors were at his mercy. Yet, true to his faith, he did not deal cruelly with his defeated opponents. In his triumph, all the persecutions of the past were forgiven. The Kaabah, the house of God in Mecca, was rededicated to Allah, and the great majority of the city embraced Islam, as did the entire Arabian empire. In 632 CE, ten years after his migration to Medina, Muhammad died.

Islam, after Muhammad's death, fell prey to the same forms of disintegration that have plagued both Judaism and Christianity. Islam became a victim of the sectarian strife as well as religious and political struggles with which Jews and Christians are woefully familiar. The multiple manifestations and conflicts within the Christian community are mirrored in the Islamic community. Our disillusionment with Islam springs usually from the forms of Islam that gain notoriety and political ascendancy. In some of its manifestations, Islam has become an ugly and tragic religion, again similar to some of the tragic manifestations of Christianity and Judaism. I am reminded of the comment of Mahatma Gandhi who said, "I would have been a Christian had it not been for Christians." The same might be said of Islam and Judaism.

Muhammad was a reluctant genius of a new emerging religious culture. While still living in Mecca the first time, Muhammad became consumed by a sense of divine presence in which he said that an angel commanded him to "recite." Muhammad resisted this call and persisted in refusing to do so until God's presence, the presence of Allah, became so overpowering that he found himself reciting the words from Allah, as if he were powerless to do otherwise. The result is the Qur'an which means "recitation" in Arabic. This revelation of God to the Arabs was similar in significance to the revelation to Moses on Mount Sinai when God delivered the

Torah to Moses. In the case of Muhammad, the Qur'an was revealed to Muhammad verse by verse over a twenty-three-year period. The revelations were a painful experience. Muhammad is reported to have said in his later years: "Never once did I receive revelation without feeling that my soul was being torn away from me."

Muhammad found this revelation of God to be intense and fraught with enormous stress. Muhammad believed that he was bringing the Word of God to the Arabic people in their own language. This Word of God, known as the Qur'an, was as significant to Arabs and Islam as Jesus is to Christianity and as central as the Exodus and the Torah are to the Jews. To be more specific, Muhammad recited the Qur'an as it was delivered to him. The Islamic religion was literally formed as the Qur'an was being delivered to Muhammad. Muslims learned it by memory and others wrote it down. This "word of God" became the centering force for the Arabs. Neither Muhammad nor Jesus nor the Buddha ever wrote anything down. Their words were captured first in oral tradition and recorded later by their followers.

Like Jesus, Muhammad was not trying to establish a new religion. Muhammad recited as one compelled to bring the revelation of the one God, the God of the Jews and the Christians, into focus for the Arab people in their own language. In a sense, the Arab people gained religious and political legitimacy because Islam became the uniting force within the tribal culture and traditions of the diverse Arab peoples.

The history and character of Islam have been largely interpreted by Christians and Jews over against their own religious traditions. Religious competition and even conflict have prevailed over most attempts to achieve religious understanding. If Christians and Jews and Muslims can set aside their religious conflict long enough to meet one another in good faith, they may learn that another religious tradition poses no intrinsic threat to their religious commitments. Muhammad saw himself in the lineage of prophets from Abraham to Jesus, but, as the medium through which God spoke in Arabic, he became for Muslims the "messenger of God."

As with Christians and Jews, the preoccupation of Muhammad and of the Qur'an was not to establish that God exists. Allah, the Arab word meaning "the god," was assumed to be the Creator of heaven and earth and believed to be the same God worshipped by Christians and Jews. Arab-speaking Christians also refer to God as Allah. The Qur'an reminds people that they are the creation of God and they exist to serve the will of God. Muhammad believed that our chief moral failure is to live our lives as though we are independent of Allah, thinking that our successes and our achievements are personal and individual.

Muhammad prescribed that the people devoted to Allah bow down in prayer five times each day. The act of praying is meant to remind Muhammad's followers that the ultimate purpose of life is to surrender oneself totally to Allah. And those who surrender completely to Allah are called "Muslims," the submitters.

Prayer plays a central role in Christianity, Judaism, and Islam, but in no religion is prayer a more prominent exercise of religious devotion than in Islam. Five times each day, a call to prayer is given and Muslims are instructed to bow down to the ground and to pray neither in a voice too loud nor in silence, but to seek between these two extremes a middle course.

The house of worship is the mosque, "a place where one prostrates himself." Muslim mosques are marked by splendid simplicity—no images, statues, or devotional objects and no choral or instrumental music. They are places of prayer, the recitation of the Qur'an, and instructions from the leader of worship, the Imam.

The message of Muhammad to his followers was highly moral in tone and substance. Muslims were obligated to demonstrate their devotion to Allah by giving to the poor and by eschewing a life built chiefly on acquisition and consumption. The world is a creation of Allah, whose presence infuses everything, a presence that is proclaimed definitively in the Qur'an.

More than in Christianity or Judaism, Islam is indeed a religion of the book. However, it is not simply a book as an object. The power of the Qur'an is in its recitation. In reciting the Qur'an, Arabs are hearing God speak in their own language. For Muslims, Arabic is the language of God. In the hearing or even the memorizing of the Qur'an, Allah is speaking. The hearing of the Qur'an is itself a deep spiritual discipline. It is a sacred event. As the worshipper listens to the reading of the Qur'an aloud, this hearing amounts to experiencing a sense of divine possession. Reading the Qur'an is not so much about gathering divine information. The reading, the hearing, and the recitation of the Qur'an in Arabic bring the mystical presence of Allah into the heart of the believer. The act of hearing the Qur'an is somewhat similar to the power of hearing the Torah for Jews. The Qur'an bears the presence of God as Jesus bears the presence of God for Christians. Reciting the words of the Qur'an or the Torah is a spiritual act in which Allah or Yahweh enters the mind and spirit of the reader and the listeners.

The introduction of Islam and the Qur'an was not without turmoil. Old religious patterns generally do not die easily. The worship of pagan deities was as much a challenge to Muhammad and Islam as it had been to Judaism. People do not set aside their gods without a fight, but Muhammad persisted in prescribing a thoroughgoing monotheism. For Islam, as with Judaism and Christianity, the worship of any other gods was idolatry and profoundly sinful. The Qur'an states unequivocally that

Allah is the One God;
God, the Eternal,

the uncaused cause of all being
He begets not, and neither
is he begotten
And there is nothing that
could be compared to him. (112)

The idea of one God, Allah, was a powerful integrating concept in a world that was essentially characterized by disparate tribal cultures, just as following Yahweh was an integrating force for Judaism. Prior to Islam, the Arabic tribes had worshipped their own tribal gods. Even in the face of resistance, Muhammad was resolute in calling all Arabs to follow one God. The notion of one God proved to be a powerful force in bringing together the Arab world and creating a coherent sense of community out of disparate and wandering tribes.

Because of the intensity of its monotheism, Islam would not have accepted the idea of Jesus as the "only begotten of God." The Qur'an makes clear that "God, the Eternal, the uncaused cause of all being, begets not, and neither is he begotten." The notion of a "son of God" would seem too much an accommodation to the culture and a compromise of God's absolute oneness. While Jesus was certainly to be regarded as one of Allah's most important prophets, the Islamic idea of one God was more nearly Jewish than Christian.

There is no God but Allah. Muhammad is the messenger of Allah, not the incarnate son of God. No divinity is ever ascribed to Muhammad. The message of Allah has been delivered to us through Muhammad, but the message is embodied in the Qur'an, not in the person of Muhammad. Muslims are to worship Allah alone. Muhammad never asked Jews or Christians to convert to the religion of Allah. He believed that they had received authentic revelation of their own.

So, Islam is, by its own traditions, more tolerant of diverse religious traditions than either Judaism or Christianity has been historically. Muslims believe that Allah has sent messengers to all peoples and the Qur'an does not condemn other religious traditions. The Qur'an says:

> Do not argue with the followers
> Of earlier revelation otherwise
> Than in the most kindly manner. (29:46)

Muhammad was a champion of justice. He believed that caring for the needy was the responsibility of every Muslim. Though the evidence is conflicting, there is clear evidence that Muhammad was opposed to violence, except for defense. He believed that "jihad" or "holy war" should be chiefly understood as a war of self-struggle and self-defense.

In Muhammad's view, reflected clearly in the Qur'an, men and women are equal before God. Muhammad seemed to have a far greater emphasis on the equality of the sexes than was present in the practice of Judaism or Christianity, even though Jesus clearly elevated the status of women. But like the followers of Jesus, the followers of Muhammad did not sustain this high regard for women.

Muhammad also believed that the revelation he received was in the lineage of the revelation to Abraham and, while he believed that Judaism and Christianity had distorted the revelation to Abraham, the Qur'an would restore the Abrahamic vision to its original intent.

Like Judaism and Christianity, Islam later became the victim of sectarian divisions that have altered the course and the meaning of Islam. The two principal divisions are the Shia and the Sunnis. The Shia tradition is built upon the conviction that the leadership of Islam may be claimed only by a particular line of "imams," all of whom are direct descendants of the prophet Muhammad. That line ended in 939 CE with the death of the twelfth imam. At this point, the leadership of the Shia was assumed by clerics who gave allegiance to Ali ibn Abi-Talib, Muhammad's cousin and son-in-law. His son, Hussein, was killed by a small band of religious opponents. His death became a rallying cry for Shia Muslims for future generations.

The Shia constitute only about fifteen percent of the Muslim population, concentrated in Southern Iraq, Lebanon, Iran, and parts of Pakistan. Neither the Shias nor the Sunnis can be described as uniformly fundamentalist, even though the Al Qaeda, with which the West has become so familiar, has Sunni roots. Fundamentalist Iran is Shia.

Some of the fundamentalist strains of Islam have interpreted "jihad" as a call to holy war. But in the Qur'an, jihad should not be translated primarily as holy war. Literally jihad means "effort" or "struggle"—a moral effort to become more holy and defeat one's own imperfections.

Rollin Armour, in his book, *Islam, Christianity, and the West, a Troubled History*, provides a helpful analysis of the meaning of jihad:

> *The Arabic word jihad, "struggle," is used in two senses in Islam: spiritual struggle and military struggle. The spiritual "struggle in the way of God" (9:24) against unbelief and injustice has always been held as primary, a battle waged within one's soul and behavior as well as in society. Islam calls this the "greater jihad." . . . The second form of jihad, often termed the "lesser jihad" and in the media rather incorrectly called "holy war," is the physical struggle of combat in defense of Islam (31).*

The current ("lesser") jihadist movement which is fostering fire and destruction certainly may find foundations for their actions within the Qur'an. Even so, I believe most moderate Muslim believers and scholars find these acts of aggression in the name of Allah to be a perversion of the authentic message of the Qur'an and its messenger Muhammad. Using the Qur'an to justify human atrocities would be like Jews or Christians using the Old Testament as the justification for taking wives to the city gates to be stoned in cases of infidelity. Jihadism as a political movement is a distortion of Islam.

The faith of Islam is built around five pillars that define its practice:

1. The confession: "I bear witness that there is no god but Allah and Muhammad is his prophet."
2. Prayer: Muslims must pray five times each day facing Mecca in the east.
3. Almsgiving: Muslims are obligated to care for the poor.
4. Ramadan: Each year Muslims are obligated to observe a month of fasting from dawn to sunset.
5. The Hajj: Each Muslim, if health and means permit, is required to make at least one pilgrimage to Mecca during his or her lifetime.

The surrender to God that lies at the heart of the meaning of Islam means that Muslims have a sacred duty to create a society of justice and fairness and to care for the poor and the marginalized. The message of the Qur'an is that almsgiving, giving a portion of one's wealth to the poor, is also a sacred obligation and that it is wrong to be controlled by an acquisitive accumulation of wealth. To put one's trust in material goods is evidence of the lack of submission to Allah. It is a grave sin of idolatry.

The revelation of the Qur'an emphasized the essential moral and spiritual equality of men and women. As Islam developed, the primacy of men became more prominent. The Qur'an does not actually prescribe that women wear veils, for example. Just as in Judaism and Christianity, in the emergence of the faith, women in Islam came to be relegated to a second-class status. Some Muslim women have fought against the regimentation of veils and other cultural practices that they believe signal male dominance. Yet much of Islam continues the tradition of male domination of religious leadership. Just so, even at the beginning of the third millenium, after 2,000 years, some Christian traditions still forbid priests to marry and do not allow women to be ordained.

Islam is not a hierarchical religion. Muhammad promoted a type of piety that grows from extraordinary devotion to Allah, above all others and above all possessions. When everyone is bowed to the ground in prayer, everyone is equal. There are no inferiors. Islam has a fiercely egalitarian ethic of prayer and giving and each Muslim is responsible to Allah for his or her own fate.

The Qur'an represents God's presence in their midst. There is no priesthood, no holy of holies, no inner sanctum to which only a few Muslims have access. Islam is thoroughly egalitarian, a religion that embraces the common man and woman. The Qur'an can be read and recited by every person. It states the unequivocal will of God. The Qur'an is a single book of revelation, which came to the one prophet, Muhammad, and through its reading and hearing, the spirit of Allah enters the heart and the spirit of the believer.

Though the Qur'an embraces all of the prophets and sages of Judaism and Christianity, including Jesus, the notion that Jesus is God incarnate would be regarded as blasphemy. Muslims are a people of their book. It is, in every sense of the word, a holy book. Before reading it, a person should cleanse their hands with water or sand and open the holy book in humble prayer. The Qur'an is to be read, memorized, and recited aloud. In the recitation, God is speaking. It is a living book of faith that inspires and sustains the faithful. To be certain, reading the Qur'an is far more about the practice of hearing God than it is doctrine or ideology.

Islam is not a religion built around ideology. Islam is mostly a religion of practice—more focused on ethical and moral behavior than theology and right belief. Only one belief is central to Islam—that Allah is one God who has been revealed in the Qur'an through God's messenger, Muhammad. Muhammad conveyed a version of the Golden Rule in these words: "No one truly believes until he wishes for his brother what he wishes for himself." *(Forty Hadith-Nawawi)*

By being a religion of practice as opposed to right doctrine, Islam is able to focus on morality and ethics as the center of faith. One becomes a good Muslim by obeying God and bringing justice into the world. Piety, devotion, prayer, and an ethic of caring and pursuing justice sum up the way of Islam. Muhammad was opposed to compulsion in religion, and war was acceptable only in self-defense.

Today, Islam is plagued with distortion and twisting of faith just as Christianity and Judaism. And Islam has fallen prey to a fundamentalism that uses religion to advance personal and nationalistic goals. Reform is desperately needed in Islam just as continuing reform is needed in other faiths. It remains a continuing struggle in every religion to throw off the chains of the human abuse of faith that undermine religious integrity. It took Christians almost 1500 years before it went through an institutional transformation on the scale of the Protestant Reformation. Islam is about 1400 years old and history waits to see if Islamic leaders will emerge that are able to reclaim and to proclaim the centrality of peace as the defining and dominant dimension of Islam.

The Qur'an certainly can be used and is used by radical Muslims to justify brutality and killing even as the Jewish and

Christian scriptures can be used to do the same. The holy book of Islam was given through Muhammad over a period of more than twenty years. The issue, then, is not whether certain passages can be found that may be interpreted, for example, as grounds for discriminating against women or justifying brutal behavior. If Jews or Christians followed the codes of Deuteronomy literally, they could also be used to justify human brutality, killing women and children, just as the writings of Paul were used to justify human slavery. But the larger spirit of each of these religions also reflected in their sacred writings points the faithful toward grace, compassion, and mercy, looking out for one another and caring for the poor.

Some Muslims even in the Middle East, especially the Turks and some of the ruling class of Egyptians, and many others in Europe and America, work to give Islam a more moderate and human face.

Even so, the demonic expressions of Islam remain prominent. The car bombing in Alexandria, Egypt, taking place as worshippers were leaving their Coptic church after New Year's Mass, killed 21 and injured scores of others. This episode was more tragic evidence that daily discrimination and dreadful atrocities continue to be committed in the name of Islam even in a society that seems to be working to become more moderate. Egypt is undergoing significant political and social changes. As the largest Muslim country in the Middle East, Egypt's ability to adopt these major changes in governance and the treatment of non-Muslims, while not allowing their society to be controlled by a radical version of Islam, is critical to Egypt's leadership in the world and to maintaining political stability in the Middle East.

The great majority of Muslims affirms that the true message of Islam is a call for justice, fairness, moderation, compassion, and forgiveness. A smaller minority of Muslims want to try to reinstate a "pure" tradition in the language of the Ayatollah Khomeini of Iran to unite government and religion and to establish a state governed by adherence to Islamic law and enforced religious practices. Still others are secularists for whom Islam is a cultural heritage but bears no obligations in the conduct of modern life.

I have been reminded by my friend, an Egyptian Christian physician, Sabry Gabriel, who grew up in a majority Muslim society, that much of the Muslim world is very intolerant and profoundly prejudicial toward Christians. He related personally his experience of deep religious prejudice and, even as a Christian, he was required to study and to memorize the Qur'an in school. We should not be naïve or unrealistic about the challenges that some Muslim societies face. Like other religions, Islam should not be given a pass on religious prejudice or abuse perpetuated by the religious majority.

No religious group has a right to force other persons to adopt its religious faith through intimidation, threats, or acts of violence. Persuasion, yes. Coercion, no. We have to acknowledge that there is great tension in the Muslim world between more moderate voices who wish to focus on Islam as a religion of peace and the strident voices who believe the goal of converting nonbelievers justifies any means.

Believers of all faiths are left in the quandary of seeking to determine how they will interact with people who hold devoutly different beliefs. That quandary intensifies whenever a majority religion intimidates or acts with prejudice and hostility toward people of minority faiths. The answer to our quandry, I believe, does *not* lie in simple capitulation, or accommodation to whatever the majority believes. It should not be so for Christians, or Muslims, or Jews. The answer does *not* lie in tacitly blessing evil or hostile behavior or disregarding the malicious treatment of others in the name of God. The answer does *not* lie in hoping that believers in other faiths will go away, blind toward those who are devoted to other religious traditions. The answer, which I will discuss further in Part III of this work, surely does *not* lie in preemptive killing out of a fear of being killed. In sum, the answer does *not* lie in responding toward religious prejudice with more religious prejudice.

Facing these real dilemmas so vividly described by my physician friend will require an answer of a different order. If we are to construct a pathway of hope that can connect our very different religious histories, we will have to put aside exclusivity in favor of mutual respect. It will not be an easy pathway to build. We will have to replace narrowness and religious bigotry, which haunts all of our traditions, with a new measure of compassion. At a minimum, we must become able to listen and to affirm the human value of a person whose life story is shaped by a different religious commitment. A pathway of hope will require that we embrace peacemaking over war-making. Unless we can build new pathways, our divergent religious cultures are likely to become increasingly violent.

Islam is a rapidly growing religion throughout the world. Still, a sympathetic rendering of Islam need not discount its malicious manifestations, but neither should we define the Islamic faith by those manifestations. We are often inclined to characterize those whose beliefs have been shaped by a different religious history and tradition as the enemy. We seem to be most fully together when we can assemble in resistance to another people who believe differently than we.

Tolerant and peace-loving Muslims, who exist in great numbers throughout the world, surely suffer from the evil and tragic deeds of Muslims who are militant, intolerant, and bent on violence. Tolerant and devout believers in every faith, including Islam, must find the courage to speak out against religious evil. Unless we do so, we will not be able to create conversations that have integrity. A true Muslim, according to the Islamic faith, is one who submits himself or herself to Allah and attempts to live in accordance with Allah's will. For a person who is devoted to being a true Muslim, it can be a small step to be deceived into believing that defending the name of Allah by seeking to destroy those who are not devoted to Allah is a righteous act.

In her insightful and persuasive work, *The Trouble with Islam Today*, Irshad Manji, a Muslim journalist writes, "If we don't speak out against the imperialists within Islam, these guys will walk away with the show. And their path leads to a dead end of more vitriol, more violence, more poverty, more exclusion. Is this the justice we seek for the world that God has leased to us? If it's not, then why don't more of us say so publicly?" Irshad Manji speaks for millions of Muslims.

For Christians, Muslims, and Jews, righteous killing should be considered an oxymoron. It is a human contradiction. We should remember that, in its origins, Islam was not principally a religion of the law. It was more a religion of ethics, of religious and moral practice, promoting individual piety and prayer, concern for the neighbor, especially the poor, and a religion whose holy word, the Qur'an, was believed to complete the revelation of the Torah and the Christian gospel. Between the eighth century and the thirteenth century (the period of the Abbasids), Islamic law, known as Sharia, became formalized into a structure of comprehensive legal concepts. And during this same period, Islam was also transformed from a solely Arabic religion into a world religion. Islamic law, like Judaic law or Christian moral codes, should not become an instrument of religious domination and prejudice and the laws should not displace civil law through which nations and states govern social behavior.

The challenge for Muslims is much like the challenge for Christians and Jews. Among devout Muslims, there is a strong desire to resist the secularization of a society dominated by greed, materialism, and unbridled self-interest. At the same time, there is also a strong desire among the majority of Muslims to make faith more relevant, to modernize Islamic law, for example regarding the role and place of women in society, and to focus the faith toward the ethical imperatives of the Qur'an, that call for justice, peace, and compassion.

Like Christianity, Islam has, within its origins, the instincts to become a religion that reconciles and heals rather than one that divides and destroys. The God of Muhammad and the heart of Islam yearn for peace, not war, and call us to compassion and hope, not bitterness and hostility.

8

The God of Jesus

While we are seeking to understand the inner life of other faiths and touch the faces of God as God is encountered through these faiths, it is imperative that we look again at the inner life of our own faith. Perhaps we can peel away some of the doctrinal excesses that become more stumbling blocks than lights along our path. Christianity is misunderstood, in part, because we have migrated so far from our origins and from the light of God that Jesus embodied in the world.

We should begin by acknowledging that Jesus was a Jew. He was born a Jew. He lived and taught as a Jew. He was put to death as a Jew. Even so, from Jesus as a Jew, the vision of God that comes to us shifts significantly from the image of God in Jewish tradition alone. For Christians, Jesus changes the tone and the substance of the religious conversation. Jesus taught his followers that knowing God is not centered chiefly around keeping the manifold interpretations of the law and thereby enabling God to find us acceptable. Jesus embodies a new language for our understanding of God.

The God that Jesus makes known to us seems not to be an Olympian god of judgment and condescension, but a God who embraces children, who heals the broken, who cares about the poor, and who lifts up the peacemakers. In order to be blessed by God, the human journey is not one that is preoccupied with pleasing God, but being blessed expresses itself in looking out for the simple needs of one another. Loving God is not so much about singing praises to God Almighty as extending a hand to the weak, the broken, and the dispirited. The outcast Samaritan who lifts up the broken is pictured as being closer to the character of God than the priest who passes by on the other side—even though he was perhaps rushing to carry out his priestly responsibilities.

Jesus came into a religious world that had become preoccupied and crippled with its own complexity. Religious celebrations and entrenched religious traditions had become burdens to carry instead of celebrations of God's enduring love and mercy. The law and the interpretations of law were the measures by which one's religious devotion was evaluated. The burdens of devotion became increasingly difficult to bear. First-century Judaism, like twenty-first century Christianity, had become so focused upon its own systems that compliance with religious tradition and law had gradually become, for many of the devout, more important than living out God's presence in the world.

While Jesus as a Jew sought to bring light and hope to people who were weighted down by burdensome religious expectations being imposed by Judaism, there is no indication that Jesus ever intended to leave his Jewish upbringing. He was a devout participant in Jewish traditions. I believe that Jesus wanted his peers and wants us to see beyond the boundaries of institutional religion and to allow God's presence and God's grace to break through the barriers of our complex religious systems.

The heart of the confession of faith for followers of Jesus is that Jesus brings new light from God into their lives. Like the Qur'an for the Muslims, Jesus is the speaking of God. In all candor, it is not uncommon for the significance of Jesus' life to be eclipsed by some analysis of the words of Jesus or something Jesus did. At its heart, the Christian faith does not claim that Jesus has either said something or done something that you or I must accept or reject. Meeting Jesus is not mostly an emotional or an intellectual transaction. The disciples embody the heart of the matter. Following is the heart of believing, even though that following may have perilous social, economic, or political implications. Rightly understood, Jesus is not a God to be worshipped or the founder of a world religion to be admired. Setting up a new and complex world religion seemed to be the last thing on Jesus' mind. While Jesus was clearly addressing some of the cultural distortions of Judaism, replacing the Jewish temple with the Christian church was simply not the focus of his ministry.

Jesus' message was much closer to where we actually live. Jesus was a friend to ordinary people, some of whom might have been regarded as social outcasts by the "good" religious people. In his relating, he became for many people a new and liberating light by which they were able to understand God in a way that connected God's presence to their own daily lives. He revealed God in a new way that became transforming for his followers.

Christians have been tempted to conceive of Jesus' living and dying as a cosmic transaction between God and mankind, in which, under certain conditions, God will save people from their sin. In this cosmic drama, however, we are likely to lose touch with Jesus as a person. In these complex theologies, Jesus becomes a larger-than-life religious figure. Theological theories often change the life and work of Jesus into a cold and distant mechanism for gaining life after death. It is a tragic distortion of Jesus' message.

I believe that if we are to understand the God of Jesus, we have to lay aside much of our religious rhetoric and ideology. Jesus, like Muhammad, is not a legend. Jesus is God's word to Christians, a person who brings God to us on a human scale. The most important affirmation of the Christian faith about Jesus is that Jesus is

God with us, liberating us. The meaning and experience of liberation for every person is unique, different for the paralytic than for the wealthy Nicodemus. The bondage that consumes and defeats us is always specific.

Unlike Muhammad and Islam, the center of the Christian faith does not revolve around the teachings of Jesus and the Christian faith is not chiefly about Jesus' ideas or his deeds, or even his death. Jesus, the person, embodying a radically new way of being in the world, is the focus of the Christian faith. Unlike Muhammad, Jesus is not simply the messenger of God. Jesus is the message of God.

The disciples, no doubt, first listened to Jesus with considerable skepticism. We can imagine how they must have felt about this young stranger approaching them with words about the Kingdom of God. They were temple-goers like we are church-goers, but the language of the temple mostly belonged to the Sabbath. Religion and worship, then and now, always seem to have their own language. Most of our Sunday language is left behind when we go to the marketplace. In their ordinary non-Sabbath lives, the disciples, like we, were more focused on fishing—making the day's catch.

Christians typically hear of Jesus long before they decide to follow him. Jesus was the language of my own family and culture long before he became relevant for my own priorities and decisions. The decision of a Christian to follow Jesus is not very different than the choice made by Peter or Matthew or John. For them and for us, Jesus becomes a radically new center for thinking and behaving. Their belief and our belief in Jesus is mixed with disbelief. We follow before we know fully what following means. The disciples were sometimes bold followers, while on other occasions, they retreated quietly into the shadows, uncertain of themselves and of Jesus. The devotion of Christians, like the devotion of followers of other world faiths, is sometimes eager and explicit, sometimes reticent and reluctant.

For all the major world religions, the great masses of devotees are more formal than passionate. Their religion is serious but not life-compelling. Yet, in each of the world faiths, including Christianity, there is a smaller cadre of followers for whom the faith is the centering force in their lives. In those cases, the content and substance of their belief reshapes the crucible in which they live their daily lives. How faith shapes us is critical. A faith that is defined by the centrality of peace in Islam or defined as mercy in Judaism or defined as grace in Christianity can become a fountain of good will and hope in the world. On the other hand, if the commitment of this same cadre of devotees is shaped by some combination of narrowness and anger, by hostility and rejection, the outcome of those commitments can be dangerous and destructive.

If Christians speak plainly about the place of Jesus in their faith, it is best to begin where Jesus began. Jesus is a person of history. Christians are often so eager to ascribe divinity to Jesus that it becomes difficult to meet Jesus where the disciples met him. What we first find in history is not the Christ of faith, but a person with all the marks of the human condition. Indeed, if Jesus were not a real and honest-to-goodness person, his relevance to our lives would be seriously compromised.

Christian confessions, I believe, are misguided and off the mark when they require Jesus' followers to view Jesus as a half-god disguised behind a mask of humanity. For Jesus, the turmoil, the uncertainty, and the pain were not a mask. I believe it is most appropriate and most revealing to treat Jesus as one of us. There should be no question of his real humanity. If we are distracted by the artificial dichotomy of human and divine, I believe that we are more true to Christianity to err on the side of Jesus' humanity. The Jesus of Nazareth was one of us.

The divinity of Jesus can be seen only through the eyes of faith. For ordinary eyes, Jesus was not divine. Affirming the divinity of

Jesus is a way of acknowledging that, for the Christian, Jesus becomes the principal port through which the divine enters our lives. Diminishing the humanity of Jesus does not underscore his divinity. The divinity of Jesus is relational. The humanity of Jesus is historical. Jesus lived among the people of the street with the same needs and uncertainties, the same fears and doubts to which you and I are subject. Jesus was a person who walked alongside the disciples in their time and space, flesh and blood to flesh and blood, spirit to spirit. So, our confession of faith should not diminish that Jesus was born in history and lived beside us in our kind of world. Whatever else we say of Jesus, it should not obscure that Jesus lived in our space. He belonged to our human history.

The Christian faith goes further. The faith affirms that through this particular person in history, Jesus of Nazareth, people are able to see God in a way they had never seen God before. It is a radical assertion. Other world religions, especially Judaism and Islam, affirm the great significance of Jesus as the prophet of God. For the Christian, however, Jesus is more than a prophet; he is the definitive revelation of God. For the Muslim, the Qur'an is the definitive revelation. For the Jew, the Exodus and the ongoing interpretation of the Torah constitute the definitive revelation.

For the Christian faith, however, Jesus has defining and ultimate significance. The event of Jesus is that event of history that serves as the hinge upon which all of history should be interpreted. This event in human experience becomes the central event for integrating and understanding all human experience. Therefore, in the Christian's experience, Jesus is neither a prophet nor a god. Jesus is the crux of revelation. In Jesus, Christians are able to see what God is like and they are able to see the meaning and the goal of history. Jesus is the person of history who enables Christians to make sense of their own history and the history of the world. The relationship of Jesus with his followers was and is a relationship of extraordinary power. It is not surprising, therefore, that the significance of Jesus' life began to overshadow the real humanity of Jesus.

This historical person to be followed was soon changed by his followers into a divine figure to be worshipped. I believe that this transformation is largely a mistake. As I noted earlier, the focus of the Christian faith should not be reconstructed into the worship of Jesus. The very earliest church saw Jesus as a simple and plain person who brought the reality and character of God down to earth. The inclination of Christians has been to make Jesus into a beautiful and wonderful object of belief and worship. But, for the disciples, he was, first of all, a person and a friend who embodied light from God. In their relating to him, Jesus became the Christ.

That Jesus is the Christ is solely a confession of faith. Jesus once asked his disciple friends, "Who do you say that I am?" They replied that some people think you are a prophet—Elijah or Jeremiah. Jesus pressed the point, "Who do you say that I am?" One of his disciples, Peter, responded, "You are the Christ, the Son of the living God." Peter confessed boldly that Jesus is the Christ. Yet, over against that confession stands the fact that most of the people knew Jesus without making such an awesome, mind-boggling assertion about him. After all, on the street he looked and talked as an ordinary person. No mere review of historical evidence is ever likely to lead someone to conclude, "You are the Christ." Flesh and blood will not reveal it.

This high confession that Jesus is the Christ stands on faith alone. Christians do not believe it because they know it. They know it because they believe it. In our commitment to follow Jesus, he becomes the Christ.

The disciples did not visibly see God in Jesus and thereby conclude that he was the Messiah. They experienced God through Jesus, and in that experience, Jesus became the Messiah. It was in and through their relationship to this person Jesus that they came to the overwhelming conviction of the presence and work of God through Jesus. The attempts at historical research to validate the deity of Jesus will always fall short. Only faith reveals it. The deity of Jesus as the Christ can never be more or less than a confession of faith. It is not a claim that is subject to being demonstrated in an objective or scientific manner. When Christians confess the deity of Christ, they are asserting that their understanding of God and their relationship with God have been defined in an ultimate and transforming manner through this person we call Jesus. In that confession, the Jesus of Nazareth becomes the Lord Christ.

In truth, like the religious confessions of adherents of other faiths, Christians must embrace this confession with all of its risks and vulnerabilities. There is no logical or historical proof. Like other believers, Christians are children of faith. The Christian faith is not first about a doctrine or a set of doctrines. The Christian faith is not even about a book, even though some Christians seem to elevate the Bible to an immutable state. Doctrines appear to be more central to Judaism than to Christianity and the book, the Qur'an, seems more central to Islam than the Bible is to Christianity. More than in other world religions, Jesus, the person, is the center of belief. Jesus is the word of God. In the Christian faith, holy scriptures and doctrinal affirmations, while important and critical to a full understanding of faith, are secondary to the centrality of Jesus as the person through whom God's presence is brought down to earth.

Hardly anyone, whether Christian or non-Christian, wishes to diminish the wisdom of the teachings of Jesus or the significance of his life—not Muslims, not Jews, not Hindus. By all standards, Jesus is respected by most religions as among the most important and influential voices in human history. The confession, however, that Jesus Christ is Lord and that this person is the central event through which history is understood and one's personal life is ordered is another matter. That confession can only be made by people who have chosen to follow Jesus. Without following Jesus, the confession is empty.

Living, dynamic confessions of faith demonstrate the difference between a religious adherent and a disciple. To be an adherent means to accept somebody's system of belief. In contrast, being a disciple requires a leap of faith, which no amount of historical verification can ever quite justify. For Christians, being a disciple means believing that Jesus unveils the character of God. Jesus' life, death, and resurrection, indeed his complete life, become the Christian's primary reference for understanding the meaning of his or her own life.

The God of Jesus is a God of relationships. Knowing God is not chiefly an intellectual experience but an experience of becoming aware of our inner connectedness to God. In this sense, God is personal. God is not a person in the anthropomorphic sense of flesh and blood. When we describe God as personal, we are conveying that God's spirit belongs to each of us, believers and unbelievers alike. God is not a remote figure simply standing apart from us, but our innermost being bears the imprint of God's presence. Each of us is made in God's image. Without that presence, we would be no more than one more clod of clay adrift in the universe. God's presence transforms us from clay to persons. In that deep and profound sense, God is personal.

Also, by personal, we mean that God's clearest word was not spoken, but lives. Jesus is the new language of God. God's clearest word was one of us. Jesus, the person, is the clearest word from God. Christians believe that religious words and pious affirmations, that well-crafted doctrines, and even sacred writings cannot bear fully God's real presence. Only flesh of our flesh and blood of our blood can open the human heart to God's heart. Our knowledge of

God is not head knowledge. It is person knowledge. The Christian knows God best by meeting Jesus.

The Christian faith also speaks of God as spirit. In part, speaking of God as spirit is a means of helping us guard against the danger of molding God into our own image. We have noted before that people are taken with the conditions of space and time. Real things seem to be spatial and they exist in time. Not so with God. God does not exist somewhere in space and, in the Christian view, God is not to be found "out there" in time and space. Therefore, heaven, God's abode, is not to be located in a remote corner of the universe. God is spirit and spirit transcends spatial and temporal boundaries. Our frail human language again betrays us. We, in a manner of speaking, ascribe time and place to God as when we say, "God is in this place." It would be more accurate to say, "This place is in God." Speaking of God as spirit means that God transcends the human categories of time and space. God is everywhere without being anywhere. In simplest terms, spirit means that "whereness" does not apply to God.

But, we should take another step. In reality, the Christian faith teaches us that "whereness" does not define us either. Our inclination is to define our lives by "where" we are and by the number of years between our birth and death—our time. Listening to Jesus teaches us to see ourselves differently. When you look at a person in space and time, what you see is what I refer to as "a region of behavior." But to identify or limit a person to what you can see and touch in time and space misses the most important aspects of their being here. Who we are is not what you see. And the person we experience when interacting with one another is far greater, far more complex, far more interesting, far more enduring than what we see. We are not mostly objects of flesh and blood. We are a constellation of relationships. Knowing whom you love and what you fear is far more basic to understanding who you are than knowing your height or your weight or your birthday. Birth relationships are more important than birthplaces.

The most prominent description of God in human language for Christians is the biblical phrase, "God is love." This description of God refers not to a human feeling or emotion but rather to a radically new way of relating in the world. In the Christian understanding of human experience, each of our lives is defined by relationships—relationships to parents, friends, even quasi-anonymous relationships such as the bank teller or the store clerk, relationships with the natural and physical world, and how we relate to the meaning of our being here, our understanding of God. Relating at its highest in the context of Christian commitment is loving.

One fall afternoon, I was driving home from work, coming down one hill and approaching another where we lived. As I began to come nearer to our house, I saw a car stopped angularly, and in another moment, I could make out that a child was lying in the street. By that time, I was near enough to stop, only to realize that the child was our five-year old daughter, Erica. A few steps seemed like a city block. She was alive and conscious, though dazed and frightened. After a brief moment, I gathered her in my arms, and her mother drove us to the hospital only three blocks away. As we waited anxiously in that sterile, medicine-scented anteroom, just beyond the doors where they examined and mended her, I learned there the meaning of *imago dei* in a new and compelling way. Erica was more than a child, more even than a daughter. She was God's nearest presence for me. She was God's image for me. She mended, and my heart recovered from its fright, and I knew as I had never quite known before that when you love somebody without condition, you are as close to God as you will ever come.

Loving is as difficult a lesson for Christians as it is for devotees of other religious groups. Love bumps up against hatred and indifference, along with the urge to be self-reliant and independent. The idea of love presumes that relating is fundamental to our being and that the character of our lives is chiefly determined by the character of our relationships. In the Christian faith, it is a mistake to confuse love as being nice or cordial to everybody. The faith that Jesus embodied does not require that we simply resolve to like everybody. Its demands are far more exacting. Christian love calls upon us to act for the good of those we like and also for the good of those we do not like. Love means caring for people for whom we may feel indifference, wrapping the wounds of people we do not even know. Love affirms the ultimate and essential worth of other people and understands that our own worth and well-being are intimately linked to the well-being of others. Our lives overlap. When another person suffers, we suffer. Therefore, as the writer of John says to us that if a person claims to love God but despises others, he is fooling himself. Love transforms every person we meet into somebody who matters. Love takes all persons seriously, understanding their ultimate oneness with the being of God. Love is God living through us.

In actual human experience, we know that love is always mixed. We are, at once, both loving and unloving. We can likely describe ourselves best as learning to love, often relating in ways that lie far below the threshold of actually caring. Even so, the Christian faith would affirm that God is present in every human relationship, even those marked by hostility or resentment. It is out of those relationships that love sometimes breaks through. The light dawns. Every meeting bears the possibility of being transformed into caring. God can speak through our relationships, and where a relationship exists, there exists the possibility that God's spirit will change the way we meet. Only the absence or denial of relationships excludes the presence of God. God lives among us and within each of us, loving and unloving alike, and God's presence gives us the hope that our own relationships can be transformed by our capacity to love.

We cannot fully apprehend the God of Jesus without reference to the Apostle Paul, the most prolific and passionate interpreter of the early Christian gospel. To know the God of Jesus, the message of Jesus must be heard not only through the gospels but from the letters of Paul, which were probably the earliest written interpretations of Jesus' presence and teaching.

Like Jesus, Paul was a Jew and remained a Jew throughout his life, but he was a mighty force in making clear that the message of Jesus was a word from God for all peoples, Jews and Gentiles alike, male and female, slave and free. Having experienced a dramatic and radical reorientation of his life through his mystical encounter with Jesus in the Damascus experience, Paul lived out his life witnessing to the revelation of God that came to him in Jesus.

Paul, a Pharisee, had been a man schooled in Jewish law. Before his conversion, Paul, along with his Pharisee colleagues, had seen Jesus and the nascent religious uprising that seemed to be brewing as a challenge to the rituals and laws of the Jewish community. Therefore, in Paul's writing, we see the gospel of the law and the gospel of grace set in sharp contrast. A man of the law became a man of grace. The light of grace that blinded Paul transformed his understanding of God's presence. Paul became a new person, a new creation, a man living "in Christ" rather than "according to the law." Like Jesus, Paul did not denounce the law. Instead, he realized that the law alone was not our vessel of hope.

Paul contrasts "living according to the flesh" and "living according to the spirit" as the disjunctive alternative for human existence. In some letters, Paul describes this alternative as living "in Adam" or living "in Christ." Living as children of Adam, we are controlled by our own selfish desires, whether those desires be economic, ethic, cultural, or sexual. It is life turned in upon itself, seeking to find meaning and hope through a whole plethora of pursuits for material and personal satisfaction, by consuming and possessing, by building bigger barns and acquiring more power. It turns out to be a life of bondage in which we become slaves to our desires and our self-centered ways. We do not become sinners because we do bad things; we do evil because our hearts are evil. Sin as wrongdoing springs from sin as wrongbeing.

Life "in Christ" is a new creation and it is a gift of God. Grace means, in Paul, that we cannot earn our way to God's approval. God's embrace and approval of us existed before we were conceived. Living in Christ is living in the light of God's eternal and abundant grace. If life in Adam results in bondage, life in Christ, in contrast, results in freedom. Centering our lives in Jesus sets us free from the control of our sinful hearts. Paul said, "It is no longer I who lives, but Christ who lives in me" (Galatians 2:20).

Paul makes clear that the God of Israel that we know through Jesus is a God whose basis for acceptance of us is not our moral achievements. Sheer grace, unfettered and unconditional, is the reservoir of human hope. This idea of grace is a revolutionary and radical idea. Paul says, "God justifies the ungodly" (Romans 4:5). The salvation that Jesus proposes for his disciples and followers today is not a mountain to be climbed, the reward for which is an eternal bliss. It is quite the contrary. God has come down from the mountain, lived out the salvation life in Jesus, and invites us to come along on this journey of faith. God is already with us. God has already forgiven us. The journey of Christians is to enter into this new creation through faith, to walk in the light which is already present. Insofar as we come into the light and become captured by the power and presence of God's love and grace within us, we can break through the chains of having to seek fulfillment through possession and consumption. We are set free, radically free, to give, to become makers of peace and bearers of grace.

Life, "according to the spirit" is a life that not even death can destroy. It is a transformed life that cannot be destroyed by something so trivial as the end of our earthly existence. There are no barriers, human or temporal, that can separate us from the God we have come to know through Jesus. The words from Paul spill out in consummate language the transformation that is possible by living in the light of Jesus' presence and revelation of God:

> *Who will separate us from the love of Christ? Will hardship, or distress, or persecution, or famine, or nakedness, or peril, or sword? . . . I am convinced that neither death, nor life, nor angels, nor rulers, nor things present, nor things to come, nor powers, nor height nor depth, nor anything else in all creation, will be able to separate us from the love of God in Christ Jesus our Lord. (Romans 8:35, 38-39)*

The God that Jesus brings to us, which is witnessed to by both the gospels and Paul, is a God who transforms the character of our present lives. We do not become Christian by adopting certain beliefs or following certain moral prescriptions. Christianity is not a formula for getting to heaven. The Christian faith changes our understanding of what it means to be a person and to be present in the world here and now. Being Christian radically changes how Christians relate to one another, how they connect with the personal, physical, and natural world that seems to be outside the boundary of their existence and changes how they relate to the ultimate meaning of the universe. The Christian faith transforms our understanding and relationship with God, enabling us to experience that our being bears the imprint of God and that God's being embraces the being of every person.

And yes, being Christian surely changes how we relate to people of other faiths. We cannot hold them in disdain and profess to be Christian.

Religion and its high doctrines sometimes turn out to be the enemy of the discernment of God's presence. The ability of religions to find common ground must be rooted in meeting the God above the little gods of disparate faiths, enabling the one God to prevail over the many gods that we nurture and worship out of fear and blindness. Creating communities of conversation can enable us to know one another better, and through one another, to draw closer to God. Listening to one another, affirming the worth of one another as children of God will make us better Christians, better Muslims, and better Jews.

9

The God of the Hindus and the Buddha

When we move from a consideration of the major religions of the West and the Middle East with which we are somewhat familiar to a consideration of Far Eastern religions that seem so foreign to our thinking, our talk of God seems to take a different turn. The Far Eastern understanding of faith and especially their God-language seem strange, archaic, uncomfortable, or even foolish to our ears. We seem to have less of a common foundation on which to begin to converse. Their language seems remote and their cultures are radically different. Even so, as the geographic boundaries steadily crumble under the weight of technology and our cultural, economic, and political interdependence, it will become more important to try to understand the religious framework that shapes some of the largest nations on earth. Even our ability to conduct business transactions or to resolve political conflicts will be affected by understanding the Far Eastern religious culture.

Buddhism and Hinduism seem a world away for most Christians. At the same time, because of the currency of our conflict with some parts of the Muslim world, we feel more comfortable and often feel less enmity toward Buddhists and Hindus. At a minimum, most of us must admit that we have hardly begun to explore the riches that may lie hidden in the treasures of Far Eastern religious traditions. My own experience suggests to me that there are no major religious traditions that have not made important and constructive contributions to their culture and to the civilization of mankind. And I believe there are no major religions, East or West, that do not have wisdom to convey and light to bear regarding God's presence in the world.

If we open ourselves to the lessons of Far Eastern religions, such as Hinduism and Buddhism, we are likely to learn more about inner spirituality than our Western practice of religion often provides. Westerners are into a more structured belief system. Easterners are more into symbolic and nonverbal communion of the human spirit with the divine spirit. They know that silence may often be a better way of speaking to God than our many words.

Hinduism

Hinduism is among the oldest of the world religions with its epicenter in India, the second most populous country on earth. India has approximately one billion inhabitants and approximately eighty percent of the people identify themselves as Hindus. The chief rival religion in India is Islam, representing about ten percent of the population, while Christianity represents less than 2.5% of the population. Judaism has an even smaller presence in India. Like the religions of the West, Hinduism has also, over the centuries, come to be divided into wide-ranging sectarian movements, including certain fundamentalist groups that wish to push Muslim and Christian members within the society to the periphery of social and political life. Like Christianity and Islam, Hinduism, in many respects, is tantamount to a federation of religious viewpoints. Yet, we should understand that the purpose of every person's life is to realize their essential unity with God. The realization of that purpose is left to each individual.

Wherever religious adherents exist, they are subject to the same human fears and anxieties that seek to preserve the purity of their faith by excluding other believers. Unfortunately, religion, in all of its manifestations, often turns out to be one of the chief instigators of prejudice, discrimination, and bigotry. Hindu attacks on Muslims and violence toward Christian churches in India have been and, in some areas, continue to be a source of significant social conflict in India. These attacks were, in part, a reaction to the apparent political preference being shown to non-Hindus. These conflicts, however, whatever their origins, become living barriers to building bridges in a time when bridge building will be a necessary ingredient in achieving human understanding and world peace.

Historically, however, most Hindus have been very tolerant of other religions. The world's religions, many Hindus believe, represent alternative paths to the same goal. So, most Hindus do not believe that God belongs exclusively to one religion, even though some Hindu leaders are fanatically intolerant of other faiths.

During the nineteenth century, RamaKrishna, among the most highly respected and influential Hindu teacher/priests who ever lived, taught that a person should follow his own religion. A Christian should follow Christianity and a Muslim should follow Islam, but, for Hindus, he believed that the ancient path of the Vedas, the Hindu scriptures, remained the best. RamaKrishna believed and taught that God has made different religions to accommodate different histories, different aspirations, and different times, but these different religions simply represent diverse ways of approaching the same God. He claimed that it was only ignorance that prompted someone to say that my religion is the only religion or even that my religion is the best. That tradition of religious tolerance, exemplified in RamaKrishna, has prevailed as the dominant view of Hinduism.

Hinduism is more a religion of practice than of doctrine. It is centered on right action. Religious rites and customs are preserved in order to bring a person in accord with the ultimate order of the world. The ultimate order of things is a telling idea in Hinduism. Hindus believe that everything has an "eternal order," and we live well when we are in harmony with that order.

Hinduism is perhaps best known outside of India for its system of castes which grew out of this notion of the eternal order of things. Everything has a destiny. For society to do well, people and things should remain in their proper order. Christians also often believe and teach that if we are to find happiness, purpose, and contentment in our lives, we must align ourselves with the will of God. The will of God and the eternal order are kindred concepts.

From ancient times, Indian society has been structured into these "orderly" groups of citizens. The highest caste is the priestly caste who were called Brahmin. Following this elite social class, there are the rulers and warriors who represent aristocracy. Another class remains somewhat below the aristocracy, but is composed of master craftsmen, merchants, and farmers who are often the most well-to-do of the castes. And at the lower end of the social order are the servant workers who number about half of the population.

In addition to the highly structured classes of society that are generally accepted as the eternal order of things, there are about 150 million Indians that belong to no caste, referred to as the "untouchables," a term rejected by Mahatma Gandhi who referred to them as "children of God," and among whom the Christian, Mother Teresa, spent her life of ministry. While these castes reflect a society that is more highly structured than Western class society, that structure has been maintained chiefly because it springs from religious roots within Hinduism.

While in the West, we are inclined to caricature castes as an evil system of class structure, to be fair, we should not overlook the spiritual connotation that underlies castes within Hinduism. The castes, above all else, represent a spiritual order in which the Brahmin, or the priestly class, is made up of those individuals who have achieved a significant level of spiritual self-realization. They recognize that the essence of self is soul and not the body with its sensual and material pleasures. The lower castes are made up of individuals who have not advanced as far spiritually. Members of these lower castes have not yet overcome the rule of lust or greed or ignorance which must and will be ultimately overcome as they proceed through lifetimes of transformation toward the full realization of their selfhood. Still, Hinduism has to face the unintended consequences that castes often come to be regarded as a hierarchy of social status that result in discrimination, prejudice and even bigotry.

In the Christian, Muslim, Jewish, and Hindu traditions, clergy seem often to be accorded a higher social standing, a kind of elite class, each of these religions maintains, in varying degrees, depending on a specific sectarian interpretation, the access of all people to the throne of God. In all of these religions, including Christianity, Islam, Judaism, and Hinduism, the fundamentalist strains of religious belief tend to make the clergy into a higher and more separate and elevated class of society. In Hinduism, however, the emphasis on self-realization tends to negate the ascendant vocal authority of priests. Only the swami who has, in effect, achieved full self-realization, gains wide respect.

One other characteristic of Hinduism that is recognized by many people is the discipline called "yoga." In the West, we usually associate yoga with the physical discipline of sitting with the back erect and each foot resting on the opposite thigh, other-wise known as the "Lotus" position. And indeed, this physical posture which requires considerable flexibility and agility belongs to the practice of yoga. Still, the mental, emotional, and spiritual discipline of yoga, more than the physical discipline, embodies the greater significance of yoga. The yogi, the person pursuing the discipline of yoga, proceeds through the stages of concentration and breathing in which he or she journeys into the interior of his or her own being and loosens the power of the external world over the mind and spirit. It is a journey to the beyond that lives within. God lives within us and the God within is known in Hinduism as Atman. Communion with the God within is the ultimate goal of the experience of yoga.

Another idea that seems curiously foreign to the Western mind and especially to Christians is the Hindu notion of reincarnation. Reincarnation means that the human soul, the inner self, inhabits a human body but the human spirit no more depends on the body than the body depends on its clothing. The Bhagavad-Gita (2:17) says:

> Just as you throw out used clothes
> and put on other clothes, new ones,
> the Self discards its used bodies
> and puts on others that are new.

Human beings, in the faith of Hindus, go through ongoing cycles of life, death, and rebirth. The person advances through the cycles, reaping whatever he sows. The new birth is a product of what he has done before. It is an immutable moral law, the karma of one's existence, that we are responsible for our condition. We are not victims. We are creators of our destiny. The progress of the human soul is shaped by the choices we make and what we will at each stage of the soul's journey.

To understand the soul's journey, we have to be attuned to life's ambitions. If our goal in life is pleasure, we can seek it and probably find it. Moreover, Hinduism does not teach that pleasure is evil, only that pleasure will not confer lasting happiness. Another person may be driven by the will to achieve fame or fortune. Again, achieving either fame or fortune is not evil, but its achievement will not bring ultimate satisfaction. No one ever achieves a sufficient abundance of fame or fortune. Whatever we want, we are all subject to the moral law of karma. Our aspirations ultimately determine our destiny and, for Hindus, human beings become caught in a cycle of birth and rebirth in the ongoing search for happiness.

We can try to gain happiness or well-being by accumulating power or wealth or success, but it leaves us with an utter sense of emptiness. The only way beyond this gnawing emptiness is to turn inward and find the peace of God that lies within. Hinduism teaches us that it is not the outward path of success and fortune that brings ultimate bliss; it is the inward journey, the interior communion with the Holy, that brings ultimate bliss.

God is always within us, often unbeknownst to the individual. The goal of life with its ongoing cycles of reincarnation is to become one with God, who is always present, encouraging, nurturing, but never requiring that the individual open himself more fully to his capacity to know and to enjoy the divine within. The ultimate destiny, however, is always sure. The soul belongs to God and will ultimately only find peace and happiness in God's embrace. The Bhagavad-Gita records that

Whoever knows, profoundly,
my divine presence on earth

is not reborn when he leaves
the body, but comes to me
released from greed, fear, anger,
absorbed in me and made pure
by the practice of wisdom, many
have attained my own state of being. (4:9-10)

The sacred scripture of the Hindus are the Vedas, handed down orally for generations. These extensive texts are about six times as long as the Bible but ordinary Hindus do not bother much with the study of holy scripture. Ritual, not the acceptance of certain doctrine, are the keys to the kingdom. The scriptures are ancient, being handed down as oral tradition and written down in Sanskrit about 1500 BCE. The Bhavagad-Gita again notes that

As unnecessary as a well is
to a village on the banks of a river,
so unnecessary are all scriptures
to someone who has seen the truth. (2:46)

In times of ancient Greece, the more learned Hindus became dissatisfied with the sacrificial myths of the Vedas. Between the eighth and the fourth centuries BCE, the Upanishads were composed, representing a more coherent and philosophical understanding for the Hindu religion. The Upanishads were more spiritual and very mystical in orientation, leading devout believers to turn inward to search within themselves to find the primal ground of being, the Brahman. The Brahman is the One from whom all being emanates and the Brahman's presence in the human spirit is called Atman. The Atman and the Brahman are ultimately one.

As a practical matter, the God of the Hindu is experienced through the worship of Vishnu or Shiva. Vishnu is addressed as "Exalted One" and Shiva is addressed as "Lord." These manifestations of God are related far above the mythical gods of the Vedas. They are omnipotent and omniscient. They create the world and sustain it. It is not surprising that people often accuse the Hindus of being polytheists. (In the same manner, however, some Muslims would accuse Christians of being polytheists because of their talk of the Trinity.)

Modern Hinduism has generally addressed the relationship between the Absolute One and our personal experience of God which Hindus experience as Vishnu or Shiva and Christians experience as Jesus and the Holy Spirit. The first model is to emphasize that all is one. The Absolute One and the world are completely one. They are what philosophers call "monists." A second model interprets the Absolute and the world as completely separate, what philosophers refer to as "dualism."

The third model is closer to how Christians have tried to interpret the Trinity and the relationship between Jesus and God. The Absolute and the world are one in essence. The Brahman, or Absolute One, is none other than the personal God we experience and the worship in the temples of Vishnu or Shiva is ultimately an expression of our devotion to the infinite and Absolute One.

In modern Hinduism, beyond the Vedas and the Upanishads, the holy writing with the most power and influence is the Bhagavad Gita, the Song of the Exalted One, which I have already quoted. The 700 verses of this poem are the most influential holy scripture of India, sometimes called the "gospel" of Hinduism. The poem is one of the great ethical documents of mankind. Though nondogmatic, it offers an ethos of living with a moral orientation of doing one's duty in the world without expectation of reward—a commitment to live beyond greed and self-centered acquisitiveness.

The Bhagavad Gita offers three classical ways of salvation: One, the way of knowledge, overcoming ignorance through meditation and study; two, the way of works, including religious and social action; three, the way of the love of God, accessible even to the lower castes or the untouchables. The Bhagavad Gita is a book of great wisdom for all who would learn of God.

A great champion of overcoming tensions among religions and breaking down the power of castes, Mahatma Gandhi (1869–1948) was a leader of political, social, and religious renewal and reformation without violence. His resolute commitment to nonviolence—resisting tyranny through civil disobedience—enabled him to become a forceful political and spiritual leader in achieving Indian independence from British domination. He also wanted people of all religions in India to live together peacefully, recognizing that ultimately there is only one God. His ethical principles, guided by both to the Bhagavad Gita and Jesus' Sermon on the Mount, identified seven modern social sins to be overcome:

> *Politics without principle.*
> *Business without morality.*
> *Wealth without work.*
> *Upbringing without character.*
> *Science without humanity.*
> *Enjoyment without conscience.*
> *Religion without sacrifice.*

Mahatma Gandhi believed that there can be no peace or social justice within societies until we achieve peace and social justice among religions.

In contemporary times, Hinduism has come to be more tolerant of religious diversity than many of the Middle Eastern expressions of Islam. Yet, even in this century, many Muslims in India experience discrimination. It should be expected that when episodes of discrimination or oppression occur, the victims of such treatment will find themselves drawn to the rhetoric of radical Islamists. The terrorist attacks in Mumbai in 2009 reflected the undercurrent of seething hostility between Pakistan and India, but in many cases, the religious differences are being exploited by political leaders.

While extremists exist within the Hindu faith, a majority of the Hindu people in India and the constitutional government embrace a more pluralistic view of religion. Even though there are some Hindu nationalists who would wish to purge India of Muslims, the larger face of Hinduism is a force for religious tolerance in the country. The religious right in India, known as the Hindutva Movement, remains a vocal but distinct minority. The ruling party of India, the Congress Party, has resisted the efforts of the more fundamentalist Hindus to integrate politics and religion. The culture wars between India and Pakistan are both religiously and politically inspired and, to make matters even more unsettling, both countries possess nuclear weapons. The result is a version of a Cold War between two countries with periodic flashes of violence.

In its origins, Hinduism itself is among the world's least violent religions in belief and practice. Yet, cultural conflicts and political manipulation move some followers of Hinduism toward an evil blend of violence and faith, one more piece of evidence that we must reach out to establish dialogues in order to secure a better way of being together as human beings embracing different visions of God. Mahatma Gandhi was both right and courageous to say to the Indian people and to the world that we cannot

achieve either global peace or true social justice until we have
achieved peace and social justice among the world's religions.

Buddhism

The religions of the world are often shaped by certain historical
figures who become like shafts of light dividing past from present,
such as Abraham, Moses, Jesus, Muhammad, and Gautama the
Buddha. Along with Jesus, the Buddha is the religious figure in
human history who is most frequently represented in paintings,
sculptures, and historical references.

Christianity was born amidst the Jewish tradition; Buddhism
was born amidst the Hindu tradition. Buddhism, like Christianity
and Judaism, did not emerge as a sophisticated theological system.
Like Hinduism, Buddhism began in India, arising from the struggle
with suffering and evil from which a rich young prince, Siddhartha
Gautama, sought refuge. Though he was a faithful Hindu,
Gautama was deeply disturbed by the ravages of pain and
suffering, by aging, sickness, and death all around him. He was
virtually traumatized by the overpowering sense that everything
seemed to be transitory and ultimately to end in suffering. The
search for liberation from suffering drove the young Gautama to
leave his family, his home and his life of relative riches and certain
nobility to search for a higher and better way.

At the age of twenty-nine, Gautama embarked upon a life of
poverty. For about six years, he engaged in wide-ranging ascetic
practices of fasting and renunciation of worldly goods in search of
peace. He did not find peace in the ascetic way. Moving beyond
an intensely austere, ascetic life, he withdrew to a river and practiced meditation until he, at last, experienced enlightenment.
Through this redemptive, liberating enlightenment, Siddhartha
Gautama became the Buddha, the "awakened one" or the

"enlightened one." He awakened to the path of liberation from suffering. He sat under the "Bo tree," short for "bodhi" which means "enlightenment," for forty-nine days captured by the sheer bliss of enlightenment, after which he embarked upon his life's journey to serve mankind.

The Buddha taught "four noble truths" that served as answers to the questions that drove Gautama into the wilderness and that burden all humankind.

1. Gautama asked "what is suffering?" The answer of the enlightenment is that life itself with its loss and hurt, with aging, sickness, and death, constitutes the existential experience of suffering, the one problem that is universal to humankind.

2. In response to the question of how suffering arises, with which Gautama struggled, the Buddha, "the enlightened one," declared that suffering results from clinging to our selfish desires, which produce greed, avarice, and hatred, and yield a debilitating cycle of rebirth.

3. The third noble truth of "the enlightened one" is that we can escape suffering only by giving up our selfish craving. Only by giving up our desires can we escape the consequences of our actions, both good and evil, and break the cycle of rebirth.

4. The fourth noble truth prescribes the eightfold pathway to achieving Nirvana. This pathway includes:

(1) Right thinking—focusing our minds toward right understanding.

(2) Right intent—tuning our hearts and minds with single-mindedness toward the goal of enlightenment.

(3) Right speech—speaking kindly and speaking truth. Slander and gossip are the antithesis of right speech.

(4) Right conduct—moving away from selfish behavior toward charity and kindness.

(5) Right livelihood—engaging in work that promotes life, that builds up rather than tears down.

(6) Right effort—willing what is good. The disciples of the way of the Buddha had to work out their salvation, developing virtues beyond their selfish passions.

(7) Right mindfulness—ignorance, not sin, is our problem. Suffering is overcome by recentering our thinking, becoming more self-aware of our inner being, allowing the mind to conquer selfish desire and fear.

(8) Right concentration—releasing desire, focusing intently, meditating, experiencing the world in a new way that transcends the delusions of the selfish cravings that have imprisoned us.

While certainly not setting out to establish a formal religion, Gautama, who became the Buddha, rejected the foundations of the old Indian religion of Hinduism along with the authority of the Vedas, the Brahmins, and their sacrifices.

It is also important to note that the Buddha did not regard himself as divine and he left no writings. He was a teacher, believing that every individual has to work out their salvation through the pursuit of enlightenment. Otherwise, they remain captive to an endless cycle of suffering.

Though Gautama may not have set out to establish a religion, Buddhism has certainly emerged in Far Eastern history and culture as a major world religion. Buddhism also has been a prominent presence in America. Buddhism offers salvation or liberation from a life of suffering. The Buddha found redemption—salvation— through contemplation and meditation. He was not seeking to spell out a new religious set of doctrines or a comprehensive philosophy. Instead, he offered hope and peace through a new pathway of salvation. Salvation is ultimately liberation from suffering through a self-transcending life of meditation—letting go of the material, the physical, and the emotional preoccupations that control us.

Like other religions, Buddhism developed in two principal schools of followers. The Theravada School of Buddhism emphasizes the actual teachings of the historical Buddha. The Mahayana School emphasizes the living Buddha, the Buddha who is our continuing refuge as we face life's sufferings. It is a form of the Mahayana School that we have come to know as Zen Buddhism, especially in Japan and in America.

Following his enlightenment, the Buddha spent the rest of his life in an arduous ministry fostering in the lives of others an enlightened path by which they could be set free from their self-centered and acquisitive lives, the root source of suffering. The way to Nirvana, the state of being that may be fairly thought of as oneness with God, is neither through self-gratification or self-rejection. It is nearer to the idea of self-transcendence—our consciousness becoming one with the cosmic consciousness. Moving from a life driven by desire and craving for pleasure or success, the disciples of the Buddha have obligations to which they must be subject if they are to achieve well-being. Those universal obligations constitute a global ethic that includes living in accord with the promise not to kill, not to steal, not to lie, not to engage in sexual promiscuity, and to abstain from intoxicating drinks.

The Buddhist religion was originally a monastic community, made up of the followers and students of the Buddha. In its early days, it was a way of salvation experienced by an elite group of monks whose lives were transformed by disciplined meditation to achieve an ultimate state of self-transcendence known as Nirvana.

Gradually, however, this path of salvation from a world of suffering was changed into a mass religion focused on developing and helping others develop a life of compassion and living beyond egocentric desires. The Buddha rejected the Hindu system of castes, believing that enlightenment was possible for anyone, whatever their station in life. Buddhism as a religion of the masses spread throughout Asia and manifests itself in many different forms. In general, the priestly class of monks observe the ways of Buddha with rigor and intensity. The masses participate through ceremony and ritual, being called to live according to the global Buddhist ethic of respecting the integrity of life and prosperity, speaking truthfully, and respecting the sanctity of marriage.

In addition, the Buddhist seeks peace and salvation through the process of thoughtful reflection or meditation, in which we withdraw from the frenzied activities that consume us, calm ourselves, and look deeply inward. Through the intensity of contemplation, we begin to work out our own salvation. This journey of inwardness leads us to be mindful of our inner lives and moves us away from the frantic preoccupation with daily routine to a quiet life of understanding and love. Disciplined devotion to the life within and profound compassion for others emerge as the essence of Buddhism.

In my own experience of visiting Buddhist temples, I was at first astonished by the seemingly unending flow of the masses into the temples. While the large numbers of people outside the temple might be milling about in quiet conversations with occasional tourists disrupting the sanctity of the environment with flashing cameras, the temple within glistened with flickering candles, beckoning to all who enter to listen for the inner light, draining away the tensions and conflicts for those who enter humbly for reflection and contemplation. For those who enter, worship is not a passive experience of receiving instruction from a master teacher of the Buddhist way, but an active inner experience. The devotee enters into a mindful state of deep meditation, a kind of intensive self-discipline, leaving at least for this sacred moment, the traffic of daily activities and commerce to take refuge in the transcendent experience of the Buddha. In worship, devotees are seeking a recentering in order to achieve an inner peace with which to confront the worldly conflicts that so often consume people. In my experience, I found that it was not possible to enter the temple reverently in purposeful silence without experiencing some sense of being emptied of life's troubles and difficulties. Outside the temple, many people may congregate. Inside the temple, the worshipper finds an intense solitariness of disciplined meditation, yielding the redemption of peace and inner strength and release from the diversions of selfish cravings.

In the Buddhist religion, the language of God differs from our own. There is no doctrine of an external God as Creator or King. But we need not think of them as ungodly. The kingdom of God is within and we meet God, using Western language, or experience Nirvana, using Buddhist language, through that deep and profound journey inward, letting go of our consuming desires and selfish pursuits.

Buddhism is the Eastern religion of greatest prominence in America and European countries. In the societies measured by achievement and material success, which so characterize the West, many individuals have been drawn to the reflective wisdom of the Buddha. In Buddhism, we don't have to go to a heaven somewhere to find lasting happiness. In fact, there is not a heaven located somewhere out there to be found. In Buddhism, peace already exists within. The human journey is about finding that center of peace that lies within. Salvation is present. It means waking up from the daze of our ordinary existence. The follower acts, through rigorous discipline, to discover the peace within that has always been present. Every person is innately a "buddha." Our sense of inner peace is being obscured by pain and suffering. Disciplined meditation and contemplation enable the human consciousness to become one with the cosmic consciousness.

There is wisdom and compassion to be learned from Buddhists and Hindus and, while they seem to walk radically different paths than we, there may be far more common ground than our culture or our own religious commitments might lead us at first to believe. Jesus taught his disciples that the Kingdom of God is within. The Buddha also taught his followers that the path to salvation involved taking that long journey inward.

10

The God of Confucius and Lao Tze

In the West or the Middle East, one is typically either a Christian, Jew, or a Muslim. Belonging to one religion presumes that one does not belong to another. Exclusivity is built into our religious expectations. In China, it is different. In Chinese religion, the actual practice of religion may and often does include elements of Buddhism, elements of Confucianism, and elements of Daoism as well as other systems of belief. Being a Confucian does not rule out being a Buddhist. Even being a Christian does not rule out being a Daoist. In addition, there may be local religious practices and rituals that also remain a part of the life of Chinese men and women regardless of religious identity. Tradition, more than doctrine, is central to Chinese culture and religion. Exclusivity among religions is quite foreign to the Chinese culture. Therefore, the toleration of diverse and even conflicting religious viewpoints is far more common in the East than in the West. Even those individuals who convert to a Western religion such as Christianity often maintain the practices and rituals associated with their ancient Chinese religion and culture. Maintaining those practices is not thought to be unfaithful or disloyal.

The rituals of ancient religions have been absorbed into the culture and have become a natural component of civilized society.

As we look closely at Chinese religions, we also gain the sense that these faiths are more akin to ethical systems than theological systems. Buddhism, which was described earlier, found its way into China from India. Buddhist temples are now commonplace in China and Tibet. The religions more indigenous to China are Confucianism and Daoism, each of which has maintained a deep and profound influence on Chinese culture. In the case of all three of these religions, finding and developing a new way and a better way of being present in the world are the focus of belief. The religions are focused far more on living well than on how to gain a future reward. Life is not about going to heaven. It is about finding a heavenly existence here. Furthermore, these faiths are not chiefly about defining a set of doctrines that its adherents are asked to adopt. They are more concerned with the behavior of their adherents. Consequently, the actual beliefs of the different religions blend into one another and the wisdom of one religion is not necessarily in conflict with the wisdom of another.

Like religions of the West and the Middle East, the springboard of Far Eastern religions is the cauldron of evil and conflict with which we as human beings and societies are continually coping. All our religions are born amidst the wrenching burdens of conflict and hurt. Our lives east of Eden are toilsome and troubled, and whether East or West, human pain is the common ground within which our devotions are bred. The problems of pain and suffering, more than any other human experience, are the wellspring of religious devotion.

In the case of China, the competing kingdoms in this vast land were in constant warfare. Warring princes made life miserable for the people. The constant crisis of aggression among warring factions led to the longing for a better way. Ultimately, the better way, which was advocated by seers such as Confucius and Lao Tze, shared much in common with the ways of Jesus as well as Muhammad's commitment to seeking peace and accord among Bedouin tribes. We have already addressed how the Buddha proclaimed a new "enlightened way." It is worth tracing how Confucius and Lao Tze interpreted the potential of humankind to find a way beyond the hardship and hurt of conflict and social evil.

Confucius

Confucius lived 500 years before Jesus, from 551 BCE to 479 BCE. Named Kong Qiu at birth, he came later to be referred to as Kong Fuzi, "our Master Kong." In the West, we know him as Confucius.

Confucius believed that if people were to live well, that is to find a path of harmony and moving beyond warring and human conflict which had become so common with the Chinese provinces, they had to align themselves with the "Way of heaven." Here the language of God takes another turn. The idea of the Way of heaven in Confucian thought is roughly equivalent to the Christian idea of God or the Brahman in Hindu thought. The Way of heaven is the ultimate reality underlying the world order, including human life. Achieving the good life is ultimately about attuning ourselves to the Way of heaven. Confucius is not proclaiming a kingdom of heaven to be realized in the future. Heaven is already present and Confucius, through his wisdom and his teaching, is seeking to bring the Way of heaven down to earth and to make that way relevant to human interaction.

We should not think of Confucius as an angry prophet condemning society and proclaiming the Way of heaven on the street corner or as an ascetic withdrawn from the daily activities of human affairs. Confucius was very much a man of the world, a very social person active in the affairs of the state. He thought of himself as an educator, an intellectual wanderer offering wisdom on ethics and politics, seeking to influence the princes as well as the public policies and private ethics of the provinces. Confucius called for renewing the human spirit by refocusing human priorities, and as a consequence, developing a foundation for renewing the fabric of public life. Confucius, for example, believed that war was not the Way of heaven. He was confident that people could be taught and could improve their ways.

Confucius's teachings actually had a practical bent, calling citizens and rulers to greater benevolence and fostering more humane relationships among citizens in conflict. If people would devote themselves to the Way of heaven, Confucius believed, they could become fully human, fully mature, a state Confucius called *junzi*, a truly "gentle" person. The opposite of *junzi* is a person who is petty in mind and spirit, greedy and interested only in self.

About the *junzi*, Confucius taught that we become fully human when we behave toward other people as though they are as important as we. He said, "In order to establish oneself, one should try to establish others; in order to enlarge onself, one should try to enlarge others (Analects 6:28). This kind of self-transcendence begins with our life in the family where love and respect are paramount. For Confucius, therefore, achieving maturity or enlightenment is not a solitary journey. We know ourselves fully and become a truly gentle person by relating to others in accord with the Way.

It is not surprising that in Confucian thought, like many other great religious traditions, mastering the ego, to which we become slaves, is the key to righteousness and is central to his teaching. Confucius was confident that uncontrolled self-centeredness was ultimately destructive to the individual as well as to the state— remarkably in concert with the teachings of Jesus.

One of Confucius's students asked him how a person could achieve true bliss, reminiscent of the question posed by the rich young ruler to Jesus. Confucius explained, "Curb your ego and surrender to *li*." (12:1) The *li* referred to the rituals of thoughtfulness, propriety, and respect for elders, respect for citizens by rulers, respect for rulers by citizens, even respect for enemies. Our relationships with others should not be driven by utility or narrow self-interest. Submission to *li* means that we should deal with one another as equals. We are never alone when we act. We should remain mindful of how our actions affect others. The way of altruism, of being respectful and considerate, was the way to find fulfillment in life. We should, according to Confucius, deal with others as equals and embrace our responsibility for the caring and respect of others. The holy person is one who lives beyond himself or herself, who lifts others up and acts for the good of others. Confucius taught a "social gospel" by which an individual could become a better person and a province could achieve a higher order.

Confucius did not engage in complex metaphysical theories and did not adopt a complex theological system of beliefs. Indeed, Confucius was not a theologian. He was a man seeking to bring the light of wisdom into civic life. In many respects, he might be regarded as an ethical humanist, focused on the affairs of individuals, communities, and families, offering instruction in a way of being that would bring the human spirit in harmony with ultimate reality, or what we in the West would call the Divine.

Confucius took the rituals of traditional Chinese religion for granted, not seeking to overthrow or dismantle them. His focus was closer to where people lived. The ultimate spirit or God of the universe, to whom through their worship and ritual, people were trying to relate, could best be experienced by relating to one another in accord with the Way. By nurturing others and refraining from inflicting pain on others, we discover holiness by walking in the path of holy behavior.

Confucius was the first person known to advocate and teach a version of the "golden rule." Confucius said, "Do not to others what you would not want them to do to you." (15:24) The shorthand for the Golden Rule is the Chinese word, *shu*. *Shu* means reciprocity and considerateness. The idea embodied in *shu* is akin to another principal virtue advocated by Confucius, *ren*. *Ren* has a variety of translations that embody the notion of humaneness. *Ren* is the virtue of goodness, benevolence, and kindness. These ideas of *shu* and *ren* may be regarded fairly as the culmination and the essential essence of the teaching of Confucius. In both Christianity and Confucian teaching, being considerate and kind toward others become the defining characteristic of a good and holy person—a person who is living in the Way or living in the Word. Transforming our relationships, which for Confucius is the Way of heaven and which for Jesus is near the heart of being in the kingdom of God, began for Confucius with the family and from the circle of family expanded ultimately to the community, to the State, and to all humanity.

For Christians, Jesus embodied the Way. For Confucians, Confucius, though revered, was never regarded as divine. Confucius was honored, but not worshipped. Confucius sought to make altruism and self-forgetfulness habitual in people's daily lives and in the behavior of the state as well. For Confucius, caring, thoughtfulness, curbing the ego were the only way beyond warring and conflict, the only way to find inner peace, or to find peace among the provinces.

Confucian teachings continue to be a prominent part of Chinese culture and ethics. The collected sayings of Confucius are known as the *Analects*. Though Confucius did not leave writings, his wisdom was written down by his disciples. In certain respects, the pervasiveness of Confucian thought in China and the extent to which the ethics of Confucius have been embodied in the Chinese culture, have enabled China to be a fertile ground for Christianity and especially for the teachings of Jesus. For some Chinese, Jesus came to be seen as the incarnation of the Confucian Way of heaven.

For hundreds of years, especially during the Hun dynasty in China, which lasted from ca. 200 BCE to ca. 200 CE, Confucianism became, in effect, the state religion of China. The teachings of Confucius, committed by his students to writing in the *Analects*, became the official doctrine of the state. Temples were built in honor of Confucius and, while he was not deified, he was regarded as the master teacher of Chinese religion and culture whose presence and teaching were revered and celebrated. Confucian schools trained the young in the teachings of Confucius. These educated persons often became the aristocratic leaders of the state. Students were taught to be considerate, respectful, humble, and to act with integrity. The emperor himself was meant to be a teacher of the Way as a leader and to embody first and foremost the ethics and values taught by Confucius.

In later periods, Confucianism ebbed in its influence and, like other great religions, fractured into different schools of thought and practice. Even so, the stream of Confucian influence is enjoying a resurgence within Chinese culture and politics. In Confucian thought and practice, the needs of the individual are subordinate to the needs of family, the community, and the state. The family is the basic unit of society, more basic than the individual. Self-interest should be sacrificed for the priority of common interests. Problems should be solved by seeking the common good, searching for consensus. People should not behave in inhuman and hurtful ways. Rather, individuals and communities achieve their highest good when people act humanely, with grace and gentleness toward society, toward nature, and toward themselves.

Confucianism is not an evangelical religion, seeking to convert believers to a new religious system. Confucius was a man of wisdom, seeking to illuminate a better way of living together, and in doing so, he laid the foundation of Chinese ethics and politics. Focused chiefly on wisdom, ritual, and humane government, Confucianism has not been subject to the strong emergence of fundamentalist sects. Violence and religious conflict, for Confucius, would be signs that the participants are not attuned to the Way of heaven.

Daoism

Lao Tze (or Lao-tzu) is generally regarded as the founder of Daoism. The writings that stand as the central frame of reference for Daoism, the *Daodejing*, are attributed to Lao Tze. Lao Tze may not actually have been a person who lived in history, but nonetheless he is the person, either mythical or historical, to whom this historic writing is attributed, probably about 400 years before Jesus. Lao Tze means "old master." The *Daodejing* is a small book, unlike the great tomes that are central to other world religions. It is written in verse and consists of eighty-one small chapters.

The "Dao" or the "Way" is at the center of Lao Tze's teaching. The Dao for Lao Tze is a somewhat larger and even more theological concept than the Way that was referenced by Confucius. For Confucius, everything had a proper Way, a proper order and the Way of heaven was the ultimate order with which people should seek to be in harmony. For Lao Tze, the Way was the ultimate reality that underlies heaven and earth. The Way, the Dao, is not a personal god but the first principle of the universe which cannot be defined or described in human language. For Confucius the Way is chiefly the foundation of the ethical life and civic wellbeing. For Lao Tze, the Dao has theological and ontological significance.

In the language of Paul Tillich, the Dao is the Ground of Being, the wellspring of all that exists. The Dao has no properties of sensibility. We cannot sense the Dao or grasp the Dao through our own intellect or desires. The Dao is the ultimate cosmic order. Only by emptying ourselves of our passions and our desires and allowing ourselves to be filled by the Dao can we be in true harmony with the ultimate nature of the universe. Nature and humanity are ultimately one. The Dao is our ultimate oneness with the universe.

Confucius was far more action oriented than was Lao Tze. Lao Tze was also more contemplative, seeking to live in accord with the Dao that underlies our being here. He believed that force and coercion are self-destructive and that a person or a nation should engage in war, for example, only when he cannot do otherwise. He writes about war:

> Bring it to a conclusion, but do not boast;
> > bring it to a conclusion, but do not brag;
> bring it to a conclusion, but do not be arrogant;
> > bring it to a conclusion, but do not intimidate. (Daodejing 30)

For Lao Tze, attitude is all-important. He describes good leaders:

> The good leader in war is not warlike,
> > the good fighter is not impetuous.
> The best conqueror of the enemy
> > is he who never takes the offensive.
> The man who gets the most out of men
> > is the one who treats them with humility. (Daodejing 68)

According to Lao Tze, our attitudes, more than actions, determine the ultimate outcome of what we do. The best response to overtures of violence is to absorb hostility or "to turn the other cheek." Lao Tze believed that responding to hostility with hostility only prompted further hostility.

Daoism became far more than an ethical philosophy. Like Confucianism, Daoism became a major religious movement and historic tradition within China. Followers of Daoism developed a sacred canon of which *Daodejing* was only one small treatise.

Even now, the religion of Daoism remains a strong force within China with temples and priests and rituals to bring its followers more in accord with the Dao. Lao Tze, as the human founding figure, was elevated to a divine status in Chinese culture, making up the third person of a trinity of "Pure Ones," including "Lord of the Heavenly Jewel," "Lord of Dao," and the "Supreme Lord Lao."

Through meditation and a moral life that eschews cheating or deceiving others, doing good to others, and repenting of one's own transgressions, a person is able to achieve immortality. Daoism combines the mystical experience of the inner life with the ethical obligations of our human life in order to achieve ultimate serenity and unity with the Dao. Compassion, moderation, and humility are critical to the life of one who follows the Way.

One prominent dimension of Daoism is the emphasis on the yin and the yang. The primal forces of the universe are the polar opposites—the yin and the yang—which are present through the universe. Everything has two dimensions—the yin being the female side, the yang being the male side. The whole of reality reflects the interplay of these two forces. The yin and the yang are present in the night and day, in male and female, in summer and winter, in the sun and the moon, in heaven and earth, in light and darkness. Both the yin and the yang proceed from ultimate reality and by their interaction produce all things, including the five primary forces of fire, water, earth, wood, and metal. The harmony and interaction of the yin and the yang represent the harmony of the universe.

Based, in part, on the importance of the yin and the yang, women actually play a prominent role in Daoist religion. Women became important teachers who influenced the religion's development. They are leaders in the practice of religious ritual. There are women goddesses in the pantheon of higher beings. Men are considered incomplete without women. Religious practice involves both male and female. Women serve as Daoist priests and have been a vital influence on the growth and development of Daoism.

Daoism, like Confucianism, is concerned with the development and maturity of human beings. While Confucius wanted to prompt social action and foster active civic participation, Lao Tze counseled inaction, rejecting political involvement. He wanted individuals to identify with nature, to seek simplicity and modesty, to withdaw from political matters. At its highest, a person lives as a compassionate soul seeking to be in harmony with the Dao.

The practical consequence of the ultimate reality of the Dao is in enabling us to become fully human. Lao Tze was convinced that human nature is essentially good. Our salvation rests in allowing the Dao to have ascendancy in our lives and the evidence of our "salvation" is leading a life of humility and "yielding"—yielding to the worth and priority of others. One Daoist observed that once people insert themselves and their own egos into their beliefs, they become quarrelsome and unkind. Such seems the fate of most of the world's religions. In Daoism, religious coercion is no better than military coercion. We cannot force people to believe and to behave as we want. The Dao of salvation for the individual turns out to be akin to the Christian idea of compassion. We achieve life's fulfillment by ridding ourselves of the egotism that keeps the Dao from flowing into our lives.

I find the reading of the *Analects* of Confucius and the *Daodejing* of Lao Tze to be moving and compelling. So many centuries ago, ancients were advocating profoundly spiritual insights five hundred years before the birth of Jesus. Even those of us for whom spiritual insight has been perfected in the life and presence of Jesus, should acknowledge that all spiritual insight is a gift of God. The Way for Confucius and Lao Tze was light from God as surely as the light that has illuminated our lives, as Christians, through Jesus. The Master Confucius said to the people, "If one has heard the Way in the morning, it is all right to die in the evening." In the Chinese translation of the English Bible, the Word is translated Way.

The *Daodejing* includes flourishes of great insight into God's way in the world—the way that we know through Jesus.

Listen to his words:

> To know others is wisdom
> To know oneself is insight
>
> To conquer others is to have force
> To conquer oneself is to be strong
>
> To know what is enough is to be rich
> To forcibly press on is to be ambitious
>
> To not lose what one has is to last
> To die yet not be forgotten is to be long-lived. (33)
>
> There is no graver crime than wanting too much
> There is no bigger disaster than not knowing what is enough
> There is no greater misfortune than wanting to get. (46)

Only by bending can you be whole;
Only by twisting can you be straight

Only by hollowing out can you be full
Only by being used up can you be new

Only by reducing can you obtain
Only by having excess can you be tempted. (22)

The mysteries of God are so great; they are so far beyond our grasp that we should learn to look for a ray of light that may come to us from an ancient one's devotion to hear God's voice and to know the Way. While Christians may not find the light reflected by these early Chinese faiths to be redemptive, they should not diminish the wisdom or the insight that sprouts like a modest spiritual greening through the affirmations of these ancient seekers of truth. If we will seek God's will as earnestly as the ancient seers sought the Way, we may find ourselves trying to build bridges rather than barriers that make us suspicious and afraid.

Confucianism and Daoism represent, along with Buddhism, the most important religious traditions in China. These traditions are deeply embedded in the culture and any meaningful conversations among religious groups requires that we take seriously the social values that have emanated from these traditions.

PART III

Building Bridges

11

Relativism and Covenantal Commitment

In a world of many religions, building bridges begins by acknowledging the reality and the legitimacy of other faiths. Just as we would be better off in the English-speaking world if we knew other languages, we will be better off as bridge-builders of faith if we know enough to nurture genuine respect for people whose beliefs differ markedly from our own. The plurality of faiths will not disappear if we simply ignore them. Numerous forces will coalesce to work against treating our faiths as monolithic structures. One is the force of technology itself. The world has shrunk. It is more difficult to keep thoughtful believers on the reservation, so religious monoliths sometimes turn to fear and intimidation as a means of controlling their adherents. Because communication is instant and global, the citizens of every country and every religion are now, more than ever before, citizens of the world. Economic forces transcend national and religious boundaries. Politics are global. The religions of the world will not be able to remain in their own self-constructed and protective cocoons.

We need to build bridges not only because the forces of civilization are pushing us together. More importantly, it is the moral and the compassionate thing to do. For Christians, it is the Christian thing to do. It is foolish to think that God has taken up residence only in our own religion and will act with anger and judgment toward all others. God is the God of all peoples. God's light shines upon all peoples. All of us, Christians, Jews, Muslims, Hindus, live vulnerable lives. We are possessed by doubts we cannot confess and longings we cannot speak. All of us, in our own places and in our own faiths, are mixtures of belief and unbelief. We are in search of communion with the sacred mystery that can heal our wounds and lift our spirits and give us peace when the sun goes down. If we can acquire both the confidence and the courage to build bridges among us, God's light will surely enable us to become instruments for redeeming the religious chaos that threatens human civilization.

When we reach out to build bridges, we are almost immediately confronted with the objection that we are simply implying that all religious truth is relative. We are accused of saying that one person's religion is as good as another and that religion is all a matter of taste. Building bridges, however, need not imply that all truth is relative. It does mean that our apprehension of truth is always limited. None of us fully understands the ways of God.

We cannot create constructive avenues for authentic conversation when we simply adopt a relativist point of view. Shrugging our shoulders with indifference offers no foundation or framework for discussing our differences with civiity rather than hostility or condescension.

On the other hand, my confession that Jesus is the "Word of God" and the center of my faith does not require an exclusivist position whereby I must feel compelled to deny every other person's claim to know God. My confessions should in no way imply or be used to assert any limitation on the will, the voice, the history, or the future of God's intervention in human affairs. I can only say that, for me, Jesus is the central event of history and the person whose revelation of God has changed my life. I cannot, and should not, speak for another. Not speaking for others and respecting their independence does not suggest that I should not bear witness to the light by which I live. At the same time, if I am to bear witness with integrity, I should also muster the courage to permit my listeners to bear witness to the light by which they live.

Insecurity in our own beliefs is the chief culprit that causes us to feel the need to overturn the validity of another person's affirmation in order to be sure of our own. While we speak from where we stand, we should leave every person free to do the same. We are neither wise enough nor good enough to judge the faith of another.

This preoccupation with assuring that Jesus is the "only" name by which the "Father" can be known often reveals more doubt than conviction. Even if Jesus is the "only" name that stands at the center of my faith, being Christian does not require that we believe God permits no knowledge of God except through Jesus. Indeed, this notion runs counter to all that we do know even through our own faith. We should let God draw the boundaries of creation, judgment, and redemption. Our eagerness to draw those boundaries on God's behalf represents the sandy soil of belief upon which sustainable bridges cannot be built. Egocentric religion is no wiser and no better than egocentric behavior. It is fear and not faith that causes us to reject others on the basis of their religious affirmations.

In my own experience, I have found exclusivism to be most rampant among large, corporate religious hierarchies. Large and monolithic structures of Christianity, Islam, or Hinduism have to constantly wage battle against the inclination to become exclusive. Growing up in a free church tradition, I found that the power that is garnered by expansive religious organizations causes them to try to exert enormous control over member bodies or churches. We are perhaps less surprised when a hierarchical religion such as Catholicism acts to exert control over its communicants. We are more surprised when a less formally hierarchical religious organization attempts to manipulate and intimidate member churches.

A large state organization of Baptists in the South recently excluded a member church solely because that congregation chose a woman pastor. The lesson was meant to be: Do not behave in a way that is contrary to our interpretation of the faith. Their act of exclusion was an unchristian act under the guise of being faithful to the gospel. They, of course, were only being faithful to their own prejudices.

Choosing between exclusiveness and relativism is a false choice. It may be easy and comforting to maintain that the Christian religion alone is true and that all other religions are pagan and their affirmations of God are false. This exclusivist alternative has a certain appeal. It is simple, definitive, and clear. We have the truth and no one else does. Under this exclusivist view, if another person ever wishes to receive the acceptance of God, he or she must "accept Jesus." Of course, this exclusivism runs through other religions as well, yielding a mountain of disrespect, hostility, and conflict.

Exclusion and relativism represent a wrongheaded and an unwarranted choice. Neither of these alternatives offers a foundation for relating to other faiths in a fashion that offers a hopeful way forward.

There is a better way. As Christians, we can affirm that Jesus reveals God's way of being in the world, without denying that God's word has been spoken in other tongues or that God's way has been revealed through other persons who have also heard and embodied God's spirit. For Christians, Jesus Christ is the central revelation of God by which every other claim to know God is measured. We should, at the same time, however, respect the word that another has heard and respect the person who has heard that word. In so doing, we may also hear an unexpected word from

God ourselves. We may see new light. Seeing new light is not a bad thing. Seeing new light is never a bad thing. The fact that Jesus is not central in other world religions does not mean that we cannot and should not affirm the worth and integrity of those persons who confess other faiths. Religions, including our own, are born of human beings. We are not passive recipients of religion; we are creators of religion. Our ultimate hope rests in God, and we have no standing to make judgments in God's place.

The real basis for building bridges, then, will not be found in the false alternative of exclusivism or relativism. Believing focuses on our reason for being here and the centering force of our lives. The Christian's faith, the Muslim's faith, or the Jew's faith is about making a commitment to a life center. To become a believer does not mean to adopt certain intellectual prescriptions. The Christian's faith and the Muslim's faith represent options for ordering our lives and those options actually share some things in common. Neither relativism nor absolutism provides a productive way forward.

The better path forward, I believe, is to see that religious devotion is not an intellectual agreement to reach but a covenantal commitment to make. Both fundamentalism and classic liberalism often become caught up in the intellectual dimensions of faith. At its heart, however, faith is an act, a decision, an event rather than an intellectual resolution of competing alternatives. Conversion is not an intellectual choice among belief systems. It means making a profound commitment of heart and life.

I use the term covenantal commitment to distinguish it from more casual commitments that randomly occur in our ordinary experience. For example, we make a commitment to attend the theater on a Friday evening, or we make a financial pledge to a church or a not-for-profit organization such as United Way. These commitments are serious and important, indicating our intention to take certain actions. As serious as they may be, however, they are distinct from life commitments or covenantal commitments that alter the way a person lives in the world. Marriage, of course, is an example of a life commitment. Marriage alters a way of life for both partners in the marriage. Civil unions among gays is a life-altering commitment. And indeed, the reason some gays affirm vigorously their right to be "married" surrounds the perception of a covenantal, sacramental relationship which is included within the historical meaning of marriage.

The act of faith for the believer is the act of entering into a covenantal relationship. Covenant means bond—a bond that defines and alters a person's self-understanding, a bond that changes his or her understanding of the world, and a bond to which one is loyal. The same defining act of faith is common to all of the world's major religions. The first and most important obligation of a Muslim is to affirm that "there is no other God but Allah and Muhammad is his prophet." This affirmation certainly is not meant to be merely verbal or intellectual. The affirmation represents a profound life commitment among people who had heretofore worshipped many different tribal gods. This affirmation represents entering a covenantal relationship with Allah that alters every dimension of living.

When Moses led the Israelites from Egypt into the wilderness of Sinai, he conveyed that God was offering a new kind of relationship that would transform the meaning of their presence on earth. They would become a "holy nation," a "kingdom of priests," a "special people." Their becoming so would result from entering a new bond or covenantal commitment. This new covenantal relationship transformed their self-understanding from living in a world of slavery in which their lives were defined by production and consumption. They produced bricks, back-breaking work, in return for which they received sufficient substance to return the next day to make more bricks. Liberation changed everything. Deliverance, "The Exodus," changed what it meant to be Israelites and the change, the conversion from seeing themselves as slaves to seeing themselves as the people of God, was frightening. They grumbled in the desert and second-guessed the decision to leave Egypt. Conversion is always a bit scary. The new covenant meant that their life was redefined to be about how they live in relation to God—"There shall be no other gods before me"—and how they were to live in relation to others in their community—respecting other people's property, respecting other people's covenantal relationships such as marriage, and not coveting what others have. The new Sinai covenant challenged everything about what it means to live well here on earth.

Lao Tze was asking the members of his community to enter into a covenantal relationship with the "Dao." Only by entering our existence in a new way—yielding to the worth and priorities of others—can one become fully human.

Whether Christian, Jewish, Muslim, or Daoist, religious commitment is a sacred reordering of life's priorities. Religious devotion means making a lasting life commitment that alters one's total life experience.

We should acknowledge that people's life commitments can change and when changes occur in one's covenantal commitments, it leads to a radical reorientation of a person's life. Divorce, for example, changes a covenantal commitment. Converting from one faith to another changes a covenental commitment. Because life commitments are so weighty and have such impact on a person's identity, leaving a covenantal relationship such as marriage or faith through either death or divorce or conversion is often a wrenching act or decision filled with turmoil and anguish. Similarly, making a new and transforming covenantal commitment brings a certain joy, even ecstasy. In every case, whether leaving old commitments or embracing new ones, these acts are usually filled with passion because they alter the very meaning of one's life and the nature of one's identity.

Ordering our lives is about making a covenantal commitment. It is not about choosing between absolutism and relativism. Faith means making choices, staking our lives around some life commitment. We cannot *not* believe. We can follow multiple pathways, trying to be true to multiple commitments. But the course of our lives will make us into somebody. At the end of the human journey, we will have become some person and that person will reflect where our real commitments lay. The challenge of faith is to live according to the highest and best light we can see. And making a commitment to follow the light of God in our lives is the most personal commitment we will ever make.

Faith, it turns out, is more about commitment than knowledge. We Christians follow Jesus, not because we can demonstrate that Jesus was the Son of God. We cannot. The disciples could not. Flesh and blood will not reveal it. We can never demonstrate the divinity of Jesus or even the historicity of the resurrection. Jesus is divine only because we come to see God through Jesus' presence. In a sense, the commitment of belief may be life's greatest risk, for when we believe, we are choosing a life center, a center for meaning and human hope. We are also choosing not to believe other messages of faith. Our commitment of faith means ordering our lives around a specific defining identity that brings greater meaning and purpose into our lives. We are not Christian because we have discovered absolute truth, but because we have committed ourselves to the truth that brings us hope and a new compelling sense of what it means to be here on earth.

Respecting differing covenantal commitments is an important starting point for building bridges. If we want to enter a new era of conversation, we must both be honest about our own commitments and respectful of the commitments of others who have come to know God by other light.

In the final analysis, our ability to build bridges and to initiate authentic conversations of faith cannot be constructed on either relativistic or exclusivist foundations. All truth is not relative. Some assertions are true; some are not. Even so, our understanding of truth and our possession of truth are not so absolute that we can justify acting in an exclusivist manner. There is a better path. Being faithful is about making commitments. Making a covenantal commitment is a serious and life-defining act. Those commitments can change and mature. But we finally become Christian or Muslim or Jewish because we have committed ourselves to a light source that changes how we see the world. At its heart, faith is a commitment to make, not a compendium of knowledge to acquire or a certitude to achieve.

Moving beyond the alternatives of relativism and absolutism enables us to meet one another with a new spirit, respecting the diverse covenantal commitments that define our lives. Our commitments differ. Those differences are authentic and real. Respecting another person's commitment does not mean adopting another person's commitment. If we are to achieve peace and build relationships that bring hope, however, we must learn to share the light with one another. We must open ourselves to the light by which others live. I believe every human being, without exception, bears light from God. They do so by their very presence. The light may be covered over with barnacles of evil and self-deception, but every human soul has within it the spark of God's light. Every person is a result of God's creative hand. We need not abandon our commitments or close the window on the light by which we live in order to open ourselves to see the light that comes to us through the devotion of others. God comes to us in surprising ways and the enlightened devotion of others can strengthen the light by which we live.

12

Overcoming Our Addiction to Violence

Building bridges will require more than making commitments and respecting a plurality of religions. It will also require that we face squarely into the tragedies and ills that are perpetrated in the name of our commitments. All our cultures, East and West, have become virtually addicted to violence as a way of solving human problems. We conduct wars to end wars. We kill to stop killing. Furthermore, we often use our religious devotion as a means of justifying our warring and hostile behavior. If we are to build bridges, we should begin by affirming that God is not on the side of violence. For Christians, if the incarnation of God in Jesus is to be believed, war and killing are surely contrary to the will of God. For Muslims, violence denies the very meaning of Islam.

In America where our Christian faith is the majority religion, we struggle everyday in our society with outrage that turns violent. In a nation that is generally regarded throughout the world as the most developed, richest, and most powerful nation on earth, we seem to suffer from this compulsive addiction to violence—both lawful and unlawful. Frankly, our power has advanced more rapidly than our moral understanding.

A Christian believer walked into a crowded congregation of worshippers and murdered a physician whose medical practice engaged in late-term abortions. The killer saw himself as killing a killer. It was an act of violence to stop what he deeply believed were acts of violence. It was violence to end perceived violence. A Muslim believer walked into a barracks and killed thirteen of his fellow soldiers. The use of violence as an instrument of faith is nothing more than human evil masquerading in the costume of belief and it is contrary to the highest and best instincts of all of the world's major religions.

Violence in our society sometimes does not have such religious and moral overtones. It is often wanton and irrational. In recent years, on a sedate college campus in Blacksburg, Virginia, thousands of students on an ordinary day of class strolled across the lawn for their morning classes. In nine minutes, the fierce winds of inexplicable violence erupted, leaving that community of learning shattered, numb, and bewildered. It was a senseless loss of the young and the eager, the gifted and the promising lives of those who were surely destined to make a difference, destined to dance and to sing, to write and to discover. It was the evil act of a young man whose own life had become twisted and broken by the very world which he sought to shatter by striking against the innocent and the hopeful.

In Kansas City, an elderly woman lay dead, her car stolen by an anonymous gunman to find his way to another killing field—a hamlet mall where people strolled into food courts and searched out the latest bargains. Three dead. An ordinary day brought extraordinary trauma.

The Christian church seems almost powerless to confront these random but horrific acts of violence. At best, the church serves as a sanctuary to mourn the tragedy and to comfort the grieving.

Almost two decades ago, I sat in stunned and speechless silence as I looked at the pictures of ashes and smoke rising from the devastating crumbling of the Alfred P. Murrah Federal Building in Oklahoma City. One hundred sixty-eight people died in the blast, including nineteen children under the age of six, and more than 650 adults and children were injured. It was one of those moments we recall that paralyzes us and causes us to sense the profound human capacity to cause hurt and suffering.

The self-confessed perpetrator of the devastation and suffering that day, Timothy McVeigh, too was the victim of hurt and suffering. His inner turmoil set off the fuse to a bomb he had earlier carefully constructed along with his friend, Terry Nichols. In the wake of that explosion, innocent men and women, young and old, husbands, wives, and mere infants who were gathered for a new day in the building's day care center, were killed in an instant. The lights went out. Loss hung over the families and the city and the nation like volcanic clouds of ash. One moment people were laughing, exchanging family stories, young professionals filled with ambitions, anticipating a special evening dinner, taking a lunch break to buy an engagement ring for his fiancé. In the midst of all that joy and anticipation and hope, the blast, the rumble and the rubble left a city silent, sad, and brokenhearted. And sadder yet were the earnest words of young Timothy McVeigh: "I feel no remorse for the men, women, or children who died that day." He felt no remorse because he was seeking deranged revenge for the devastation in Waco, Texas two years earlier exactly to the day. Men, women, and children lost their lives in the Branch Davidian Compound. McVeigh decided the government was evil and that the government had to be punished for that tragedy. It was an act of political fundamentalism.

Like Timothy McVeigh, most people who do such evil acts believe they are doing good, making God's world a better place.

They are righting wrongs. The problem of evil is not only that it hurts. We engage in evil and hateful acts and words, trying to right wrongs through destruction, because we lose our way. We become victims of the chaos that leaves us twisted and half-blinded, dominated by the darkness that overcomes us within. Living in the darkness, we seek to build hope through destruction; living in the light, we find hope by redeeming the evil and helping to rebuild the shipwrecks that occur on the shoals of human fear and anger and twisted human spirits.

The violence is not new. In conquering Canaan, Joshua swept from north to south to subdue the whole country. The Israelites rushed in, killing everything in sight, men, women, and children. Only a harlot and her family were spared because she had provided shelter for Joshua's spies. Moreover, Joshua and his armies committed these atrocities believing, or at least justifying them by claiming, that they had been commanded to do so by almighty God.

Violence, everywhere. If we are to build bridges among our confessions of faith and if the church or the mosque or the synagogue is to become a source of hope and light for the victims and the victors of violence, we must confront the challenges of violence that are, in some cases, being nurtured and sponsored by the very faiths we profess. Human beings, including Christians, Muslims, Jews, and Hindus, are taking a deadly and vicious toll in the whirlwind of terror and rage that is spreading throughout our world. Since our world's religions are contributing to this violence, we have to set our sights on charting a better way forward in a world being darkened by the ugliness that is emanating from our bastions of faith.

Violence should remind us that humanity is not only the children of Adam; human beings are also the children of Cain. Exposing the ugliest strains of our human character, violence is not simply a phenomenon of 9/11 or in Baghdad. It is not simply a phenomenon in Blacksburg or New York, in Kabul or Tehran. It's not simply a tragedy spawned by the Hitlers or Husseins, by Osama bin Ladens, by Hamas, by Hesbollah or Iran or Kim Jong-il. The problem with human violence does not just exist out there in someone else's heart and soul. Our presumed innocence and our self-righteous judgment are mostly a way of washing our hands of the reality that we are all children of Cain, whether Muslim, Christian, or Jew.

We indeed live in a tinder-box world. It has become a world where hostility and bitterness have exploded onto the human scene more dramatically and more destructively than ever before. Killing in schools, killing in malls, massacres in our cities, worldwide.

As human beings and as people of faith, we have presumed to establish the ways of peace by killing in return. Neither Muslims nor Christians nor Jews can hope to end the killing with more killing. Somewhere deep within us, we should ponder whether military power and precision bombs and youthful martyrs alone will be sufficient to overcome the debilitating reign of terror. Terror will not turn out to be an effective champion of faith.

Perhaps we should begin with a new affirmation that can bring us closer to building bridges. My affirmation is this: There is no good violence. War is not good violence. Capital punishment is not good violence, and I venture to say that the notion of "holy war" is a contradiction, nothing more than a euphemism created to help us manage our guilt.

War is never holy. Surely, there are moments in our tragic and broken human history when war has been and will be inevitable. But let us not deceive ourselves into believing that war, that people killing other people, even when it seems that it is the best that we can do, is a good or righteous act. War and killing always echo our broken human condition, our failure to achieve God's purposes in creation. Because we do indeed live in an immoral society where evil yet abounds, wars, again, may be inevitable but they are never good, never holy. They may be just, that is, they may be directed toward restoring justice (I think of Bosnia, for example), but the justification of war should take place with enormous caution. It is so easy to rationalize establishing our way, our priorities, and our beliefs with establishing justice. Wars rarely create justice even though they may, at times, seem to be our only deterrent to injustice. But war is too easily regarded as the cure to the world's ills. At its very best, war contains and limits the ravages of evil, but it cannot bring redemption. Redemption can only be found in the hard work of picking up the broken pieces, embracing the defeated, caring for the enemy, and acting sacrificially to build a better order in the world.

Violence is closer to home and it is perpetrated not only with guns and knives. Violence wears many faces. Let us count the ways that human beings, like Cain, put Abel to the ground—the violence of power, the violence of prejudice, the violence of language, the violence of sexual abuse, the violence toward persons with different sexual orientations, the violence of silence, and perhaps most pernicious of all, violent and hateful religion wearing the veil of holiness. Violence wears so many faces.

The violence of power. Violence is power out of control, unbridled and destructive. It may be the untamed power in the workplace where one uses authority or position to demean and to ridicule. It may be the power of an authoritarian government.

The violence of sexuality is everywhere present. Sexual abuse victimizes more people than backstreet thugs on Saturday night—child abuse, spouse abuse, rape—sex is used to control and to diminish.

The violence of economic peril—more than half of the world's population live on less than a dollar a day. While we can and should celebrate our economic progress, it is an act of violence to ignore the people who live on the margin, for whom poverty and economic hopelessness breed gang warfare and despair. If we continue to ignore economic injustice, it will finally burn our democracy to the ground.

And there is the violence of religion where devoted Christians, not just Muslims, kill and maim in the name of God. Whether it is Islamic jihad, Jewish Zionism, or the Christian's Army of God, it is all dangerous and violent religion. It is religion gone bad. Violence is the outcome of religion that has been hijacked by fear and anger or greed and power.

While we worship in our respective faiths, we live on the edge of trauma and chaos. Our faiths may turn out to be our highest and best hope, perhaps our only hope. The truth is that violence arises from deep within us. We are wrenched and torn by fear and anger. Our inner turmoil breeds rage and resentment and malice and hostility. Wallowing in the tragedy of unbridled self-importance, we diminish, we dismiss, and we destroy. Like Cain, we kill because we are jealous and afraid.

Fear will not be stemmed by mindless brutality or raging conflict. Fear will abate and anger will subside only when we discover and commit to a new way of being together. If we are to escape the vise-like grips of violence, it will not be because we have grown stronger. It will not ultimately be because we have acquired more lethal weapons. It will be because we have been captured by a blazing new light, because we have the courage to hear a new voice and to ask one another in our diverse faiths for forgiveness. Christians need to ask Muslims for forgiveness; Muslims need to ask Christians for forgiveness.

Our eggshell world is broken to pieces—shattered, lying in crumbles, smoldering and jagged. What are we to do with the pieces?

As one who is deeply troubled by the darkness that is crippling human civilization and creating enmity among our faiths, I propose that we Christians should start where we are. Muslims and Jews should start elsewhere, at their own authentic beginnings, for they are likely to find peace, not violence, at the headwaters of their faith.

As for Christians, we have to start with the person of Jesus. Jesus himself was the tragic victim of human violence. For Jesus, violence was not abstract or remote. Violence was not a theoretical challenge. Jesus felt the sharp human assaults as a dreadful, devastating, shattering avalanche of rejection that brought searing pain and a wrenching death.

Christians will remember that violence visited Jesus in Gethsemane where he was arrested in the presence of his disciples. Roman soldiers with their swords and paraphernalia of war marched into the Garden of Prayer, violating the night. Like us, the disciples had not learned. Peter, the most swashbuckling of all the disciples, did what we are always inclined to do. He confronted violence with violence. We do it everyday. Peter's response was so contemporary. Peter drew the sword, defiantly cutting off the ear of the approaching soldier. It is our human way—meeting violence with violence, confronting it head on, holding our ground, taking on the enemy.

If we are to overcome violence and replace bombs with bridges, we must come together as people of diverse faiths and celebrate that we are children of one God. Together we should do the hard work of establishing a new way of being in the world.

First, we have to pick up the pieces. As Christians, we have to do what Jesus did. We have to pick up the ear we have severed and put it back on. You see, violence will never be the cure for violence. And there is no easy or shortcut way to pick up the pieces. We have to rebuild what our violence has destroyed. We have to heal the wounds that violence has inflicted. We have to go through the rubble and rake up the debris. We have to rebuild the buildings, light the storefronts again, place goods back on the shelves. It requires sacrifice, investment, taxing our purses and our hearts. It is not enough to say, 'I'm sorry." When Peter acted with violence, Jesus' response was to redeem the violence. Retaliation should never be our last word. God's last word is redemption. If we want to walk that path, we should realize that redeeming the violence is hard, brutal, painful, backbreaking work. Yet, if we follow the highest truth of all of our faiths, we have to begin by redeeming the violence.

Second, we have to look for ways—specific and concrete—to respond to violence with compassion—compassion for the wounded and compassion for those who inflict the wounds. There is only one cure for human rage. That cure is holy, deliberate, and willful caring, even for those who do us harm.

Unencumbered compassion that is central to all our faiths, that is, love that has no conditions, is the only way out of this death spiral of human hatred. Hatred cannot drive out hatred. Only reaching out in a new spirit to the hated can do that. Violence will not end violence. Only love that has no boundaries or conditions will do that. It is a hard word to hear because compassion has not been our way.

It sounds so foolish, so naive, so unrealistic as to be absurd. But let us hear this word in all of its foolishness simply because our old way is not working. In our irrational rage, we can kill until our planet grows deathly silent. Our capacity to destroy, even to annihilate, has reached epic proportions. Fighting will never end wars; capital punishment will never abolish crime; hitting back will never make us even. Killing one another simply is not working.

Overcoming our addiction to violence will require simple, unvarnished forgiveness—not forgiveness if you will repent, not forgiveness if you beg and humble yourself.

You and I, of course, have come to design our own brand of forgiveness. Our brand of forgiveness often sets out to cripple the one asking to be forgiven, to make that person walk with his head pitched low, "I'll forgive you this time, if you promise never to do it again."

The plain truth is that we prefer to get even. Forgiveness means to embrace the hurt, and harder still, to embrace the one who brought the hurt. Forgiveness is about lifting up our enemies, for while they may be our enemies, they are not the enemies of God. As Christians, the light of Jesus should enable us to see in the faces of our enemies, the very face of God. We may have to look hard, but we can be sure that God is there. Violence will ultimately be overcome only if we meet it with forgiveness. It makes good political theater to track our enemies to the gates of hell, and in this immoral world, it may seem to be the only way to be elected to political office. But it is not the ultimate truth. God loves every Muslim and every Jew as much as God loves every Christian.

While it is profoundly important to understand and to initiate the power of forgiveness, it is also necessary to ask what the idea of forgiveness means in the context of nation states. We should not be naïve. Forgiveness must and can be translated into thoughtful and careful acts of diplomacy and acts of national restoration.

The Marshall Act in Europe after World War II was an act of translating forgiveness into a constructive international program. The ultimate release and partial restoration of Japanese-Americans following the defeat of Japan were acts of social repentance and forgiveness.

Our present age will require that we as Christians build and rebuild our relationships with Islam. The rejection of all Muslims because some fundamentalist Muslims have behaved in inhumane and evil ways does not justify hostility and hatefulness toward Muslims, whether they live in New York, or Tennessee, or Baghdad. We, too, have behaved destructively and, on occasions, more out of revenge than self-defense, we have acted to kill innocent Muslims because they have killed innocent Christians or innocent Jews. Revenge will not be enough. We have to come together as people of faith and people of reason and seek to find and to create a better and more godly way of being in the world, of sharing the earth and all its resources.

We need not dismiss the idea of forgiveness as pious talk. Leaders and shapers of civilization must behave in the world in a manner that heals the wounds and provides a runway on which we can reconceive our lives together. The role of world religions is not to sit on the sidelines, leaving the hard work of creativity and emancipation from violence and our violent ways to the forums of politics and governments alone. Peoples of faith must speak and act, and thoughtfully, and respectfully, join in the creation of a new heaven and a new earth.

But lest we think that our meanness and incivility have created a mountain of regret too high for us to climb, I have a word of hope. There is hope in the dark shadows of our anguish. That hope is that we, like Cain, also bear the mark, the imprint, of God. And, that mark means that God is still with us and God will not leave our side. God will not leave the side of the neglected or those who neglect. God will not leave the side of the injured or those who injure. God will not leave the side of the victor or the victim, the violent or the violated.

God's revolutionary word is for us to see one another, even our enemies in a new and radically different way. God is calling us to pick up the pieces, to heal the wounds, to meet violence with forgiveness.

We will not win the war against terrorism with guns alone. Religious bigotry, which is simply another form of violence, will not be overcome by passing out tracts on how to be saved. Evangelism may be a good thing. But bearing witness in a way that condemns and judges, that disrespects and treats people of other faiths with a condescending arrogance is a sinister force, seeking to manipulate and control. Whether in Muslim clothing or Christian clothing, bigotry fuels the flames of hatred and meanness. Religious hatred is still hatred; holy meanness is still meanness.

Those Muslims are wrong who believe that they can establish the superiority of Islam through violent defeat of nonbelievers. Those Jews are wrong who believe that they can establish or preserve the land of Israel as their promised land by the violent defeat of the Palestinians. Those Christians are wrong who believe that they can establish the Christian faith by treating Muslims as enemies or by the violent defeat of our religious adversaries.

Our own inhumanity can be daunting. It seems more natural, more rational, even safer, to live like our brother, Cain—profane and vengeful, putting down those who threaten us. But we should face up to the clear reality that both violence and our violent response to it are shrinking us. Our humanity is being diminished by our inhumanity. We can be certain that the moral high ground will never be claimed solely by military victories. No doubt, we will continue to wage wars. The conflicts in the Middle East are likely to go on for decades, but let us never begin to believe that wars will ultimately bring peace or disarm hatred.

If we are to build bridges, we simply have to let go of retribution and revenge as the foundation of our hope. We need to hear a radically new and revolutionary word. The word of Jesus and, I believe, the word embedded in every faith that has heard God's voice, is that we are to love our enemies and forgive those who hurt us. Let us not dismiss loving our enemies as simply pious language. I am not speaking of syrupy sentimentalism. Loving our enemies is not a metaphor. It means to respect them. It means to hear their cry, to be mindful of their hurt and their tragic human stories. It means to be kind to people you don't like. We will not know God's kind of world until that radical revolution begins to take hold in our own lives.

Pick up the pieces. Heal the wounds. Build back from the ashes. If we can find the courage to begin to live in the transforming light of unbridled compassion, and to begin to embrace the power of forgiveness, we have the foundation for building bridges that will carry us toward peace.

13

Creating a Community of Conversation

After serving as president of a university for only a short while, I came to a powerful realization which I believe was the single most important lesson I had learned during my presidency. The lesson was this: more problems are solved by listening than by talking. A university, in particular, is a guild of bright and gifted individuals who inevitably have strong and intelligent views, and most of those individuals, as a byproduct of the profession they have chosen, are able to articulate their viewpoints effectively and persuasively. Still, the president had views as well and the differing perspectives sometimes led to genuine debate among colleagues. It was a telling example of the adage that "where you stand often depends on where you sit."

One approach to our human differences is, of course, to try to drown out other voices, especially the voices of opposition, with our own rhetoric. Talking nonstop, filibustering our viewpoints, can result in others simply throwing up their hands in despair of ever being heard. At least, that is what we hope. It is tempting for people in power, whether religious power or political power or economic power or academic power, to ridicule or diminish or to find other ways of excluding dissent. We have succumbed to that temptation whenever we talk without listening or make judgments without collaboration. Such tactics are efficient because they offer the quickest resolution of conflicting views. But they are very ineffective in their ability to resolve conflicts and solve problems in lasting ways.

Listening and collaborating do not mean, of course, simply capitulating to someone else's point of view. Problems in academia and among religions, in part, exist because we do actually see ourselves and our worlds differently. No person can see what you see or envision exactly what you can envision. But genuinely hearing an opposing or divergent point of view can sharpen our own perspective and convey that the person who holds another view or belief is an important partner on the human stage. Ironically, people in power actually become more powerful when they develop the courage to take other people's perspectives seriously. In short, talking loud and endlessly is weak; listening is strong.

I believe that this lesson is remarkably relevant when we consider our interaction with other faiths. We live in a world of religious faiths with there is far too much talking and too little listening. Listening requires a greater sense of security than talking. Moreover, listening, not talking, can become the key to solving problems and breaking down barriers that have been erected by our religious systems.

Building bridges is going to require that we become more open to the wisdom and the light of God from wherever it flows. If we wish to begin to take the barriers down, we will have to take the blinders off so that we may learn more of God's creative and redemptive ways in the world. If we have the courage to do so, the good news is that we are likely to be rewarded with new and refreshing insight into God's presence in the world.

Within humankind, God has been called by many names. I grow ever more convinced that our own religious devotion as

Christians would be greatly strengthened and profoundly enriched by the willingness to allow new and fresh names for God to flow into our hearts and minds. We do not need to be afraid. None of us sees with perfect clarity. As I encounter the wisdom of the world's religions, I am reminded over and over again that God embraces us all without condition.

In a world that has become dangerous, in part, because we have allowed fear to displace our better wisdom, one clear antidote to the violence we have described earlier will be found in our willingness to engage in open, honest, candid conversations about our differing faiths. A conversation must involve both listening and speaking. A commitment to conversation does not mean that we should dismiss or ignore our differences. They are real and significant. While I believe all religions bring light, they also create blindness. The differences in our faiths, in our religious preferences, in our political leanings, are immense. Our hope for a better future as citizens of the world does not likely lie in pretending that those radical religious and political differences do not exist. The question is whether we, as human beings in all our humanness, can reach the level of civilization that engages the clash of ideas and beliefs in a fashion that enables persons who hold these differences to exist together with a measure of mutual respect.

I am proposing that conversation and thoughtful engagement are a better and a higher road than putting other people down. Conversation does not require that we diminish, in any respect, the covenantal commitments central to our lives. If we are to survive as a human species, we must learn to replace a community of disrespect and hatred with a community of respect that can be fostered through honest and genuine conversation. The reasons to take this bold and courageous step are becoming increasingly relevant and crucial to our very survival. We face this alternative: Either we can engage our radical differences with some form of hostility or we can carefully and devoutly seek to create communities of constructive conversation.

If we are to create these communities of conversation, we will be able to do so only if both parties to the conversation acknowledge the value of the other's religious conviction. Conversation cannot begin by denying the worth of another person, including the deep convictions that order another person's life. We take an enormous step away from disrespect and toward a civilization of hope when we are willing to affirm the worth and value of another person or another group of persons, including the beliefs that they embrace.

Conversation also presupposes that people of conviction will be able to represent their convictions and articulate them with some clarity, while listening openly to the convictions of others. Conversation finally requires that we shed enough of our defensiveness to be willing to hear criticisms of our beliefs and search for an articulation of misunderstandings that will be prevalent among all parties. There are no perfect religions because there are no perfect religious people.

The modest conditions I have outlined here establish, I believe, a beginning framework for open and honest conversation. But once underway, conversation becomes its own reinforcement. In conversation, we not only learn more about what someone else believes, we learn more about what we believe. Furthermore, we are likely to discover along the way that our doctrines of belief are less important than our experiences of faith. Creating circles of conversation does not need to lead to some determination that one religion is right and the other is wrong. Conversation is not about dueling beliefs and seeing who can make the best case. It is about learning to appreciate one another as believers and about achieving understanding and a genuine measure of respect.

Catholic theologian Hans Küng reminds us that "until there is peace among religions, there can be no peace in the world." (Hans Küng, *Tracing the Way*, p. 266) I believe that a good place to begin our conversations as communities of faith is to acknowledge that God is greater than any of our claims on God. God is not the possession of Christians or Jews or Muslims, not the possession of Hindus or Buddhists or Confucians. God is not a Christian. God is not a Muslim. God is not a Jew. God is not a Buddhist. God is not a Hindu. God is above all our gods. God is the ground that makes all our gods possible. God is the being that makes it possible that Allah is God and that Yahweh is God.

Some new and important initiatives have begun in interfaith dialogue. The Minhaj-ul-Quran International is a nonsectarian group working in more than eighty-one countries. Its main aims and objectives are to promote interfaith conversations and to live peacefully within society. Pope Benedict XVI has been outspoken in his support for dialogue with Muslim leaders. In July 2008, King Abdullah of Saudi Arabia, a monolithic Muslim state, initiated a conference which was held in Spain and sponsored by King Juan Carlos to seek to solve world problems through concord and not conflict. Religious leaders from Christianity, Judaism, Buddhism, Hinduism, Daoism, and Islam attended the gathering. The Vancouver School of Theology opened Iona Pacific Inter-Religious Centre for Social Action, Research, and Contemplative Practice. The World Economic Forum has launched the "Council of 100 Leaders," a group of ministers, imams, rabbis, priests, and academics to explore the common ground among our religious cultures. And in 2008, The Tony Blair Faith Foundation was begun in order to advance the search for peace among religious peoples of the world.

These initiatives are modest and embryonic efforts for beginning conversations in a religiously plural world. As ordinary believers, I believe it is profoundly important that the conversations among devout people of faith not be left to clerics and religious chieftains. Enmities will be overcome, peace will be spawned, and good will be achieved as we encourage ordinary people of faith among local congregations of believers to begin to listen to one another across religious boundaries. Lay people, it turns out, are very often less defensive than the priests and imams and rabbis. Peace must be achieved neighbor to neighbor if we are ever to achieve peace nation to nation. Reform may more likely flow upward than downward.

If we are to engage in serious, thoughtful, and earnest conversations, it may be helpful to begin those conversations from some common threads that belong to the fabric of all our faiths. In order to examine those common threads, it will be necessary to acknowledge that when we come together in conversations with persons of another faith, we are joining voices with people who are as fully embraced by God as we. The willingness to tell and to listen to our stories with one another can potentially transform our meeting place into holy ground for all of us.

I offer here seven threads with which a new garment of understanding might begin to be woven. These threads are meant to be exemplary, not exclusive, and are meant to prompt our search for more common threads from which we can weave a larger and stronger sense of community among our diverse faiths.

1. *The first common thread is a simple one: We all have a story.* Each of our religions has a remarkable story to tell. Put differently, every religion and every person's life forms a mythology—a story that frames the contours of religious meaning and self-understanding. Our lives and our religions are not collections of facts to accept. There are, of course, facts in the world. There are mountains and streams, asteroids and dinosaurs of long ago. There are

facts to be known. So, we do not diminish the reality and value of facts. The existence of religions is a fact. But being religious is not initially about affirming facts. Every religion—a common golden thread—is a constellation of sacred stories, not facts. By becoming Christian, we are not simply affirming the fact of Jesus. We are entering and becoming a participant in the Christian story. The Christian myth or story becomes the telling account by which we make sense of our being here.

As an aside, we should not be confused or put off by the notion of myth. For example, myth was one of Jesus' most important linguistic tools for communicating the meaning of the kingdom of God. We call these myths parables. Myths are as old as the human race. Ancient societies used myths to explain the world in the absence of scientific information. Today, we have lots of scientific information, but myths remain compelling stories that shed light and make sense of our being here, sense that science alone can never provide. Myths put words and music to the great mysteries of life.

Jesus himself used the power of myth precisely because the most important realities in our world are beyond the reach of mere scientific explanation. Science can analyze what is "out there," but it cannot fathom the mysteries of what it ultimately means. Those are the questions of faith. The stories of creation, suffering, and redemption carry us to another level of understanding. If you want to know me, or I want to know you, data will not be enough. Analysis will tell us our chemistry, but it will not unlock the deeper mysteries that make us into the persons we are. To know us as persons, we must know one another's longings and passions, one another's fears and devotions. And to know those realities, you will have to hear my story, and I will have to hear yours.

The myth of our lives is what makes our lives interesting and compelling. The fact of our lives may be curious but not always interesting. The composition of our lives as persons with loves and fears, with anxieties and hopes and as individuals who connect the anticipated with the unexpected is what gives color and character to our lives. We are not a collection of facts; we are a collection of stories. We are not a collection of minutes; we are a collection of moments.

Each of our religions and each person who is religious are constellations of stories. Every person's life is more than a chronicle, more than a collection of facts that might be recited in an obituary. Obituaries may capture our facts, but they can never capture the richness of our human stories. Every religion has a history, and it is a history still being made. They have wonderful stories to tell that hearten the human soul.

We should come together to listen to one another's story. Our diverse stories represent a thread of gold that is woven into the fabric of all our faiths. Everybody's story can enlighten us and can enrich our own story. Myth and story are one common thread around which we can and should begin to build our conversations of faith.

2. *A second common thread, in every faith, it that life cannot be defined solely by the boundaries of life and death.* We are not here simply to live until we die. Whether we are speaking of the Greek pantheon of gods or the Confucian goal of becoming a *junzi*, or a Christian disciple, or an enlightened one following the Buddha, each of the world's faiths interprets human life and the world to be more than can be adequately described by looking through the window of our existence between life and death. Each of the world's faiths proclaims that human life has enduring significance and that our being here serves higher purposes. While we may disagree regarding the purposes of life, each of our faiths prescribes

that we should see ourselves in terms of meaning and purpose. We are of the earth but not defined by earth alone.

Human existence, then, is the starting point for all of us, regardless of the divergence of history and beliefs. None of us asks to be born. We had nothing to do with our arriving here on the human stage. So, we wonder what our being here means. That is the basic human question. One answer, of course, is that our being here means nothing. Some have concluded, and they believe reasonably so, that human life gradually emerged from a watery coagulation of cells that found their way to land and, through natural selection, we were programmed through eons of the emergence from lower forms of life into creatures with more sophisticated mental capacities.

Perhaps more than 200,000 years ago, creatures emerged who might properly be called human. If, however, the existence of the universe were viewed as a twenty-four hour day, human life would have emerged only in the last fraction of a second. Human life on earth, whenever it emerged, is a recent event in a universe purported to be about fourteen billion years old. We have barely arrived. One may conclude that this human species with its emergent religious consciousness is simply one more stage in the evolutionary development of the universe. Further, one might suspect that human life on earth is one of the more underdeveloped forms of life in the universe. Viewed in these terms, human existence may be nothing more than a historical novelty in the slowly expanding universe before it collapses back in upon itself. In other words, we can choose to account for human existence as one rather brief episode in a vast universe that means nothing beyond its episodic moment, and that human existence has no enduring significance.

In contrast, all our religions, in unison, account for the human episode by seeing within it a clue of why the universe exists at all.

Our religions, in unison, believe that the universe and our presence within it are more than physics and biology can account for. While physics and biology may be central to understanding the universe and human life, they alone will be unable to unlock the ultimate mystery of the universe or why, as Martin Heidegger asked, "there is something rather than nothing." All our religions face into the manifold mysteries of the universe and affirm, in diverse ways and through the languages of different stories, that the world and our presence within it serves enduring and higher purposes. We are here for a reason. That belief and commitment to higher purpose and meaning beyond the brief boundaries between life and death are one of the common threads belonging to all our faiths and around which we can and should begin to weave our conversations.

3. *A third common thread woven among all our religions pertains to the human struggle to cope with pain and suffering.* The problem of evil is near the forefront of all the world's religions. The question of how we account for suffering usually emerges as a defining characteristic of faith, and every faith offers a way of explaining and/or coping with the tragic dimensions of human living. It was the problem of suffering that drove Siddartha Guatama from his life of relative ease and fortune into the wilderness to search for an answer for human suffering.

Every religion faces a genuine dilemma in the apparent contradiction between a notion of God that is all-knowing and all-powerful and also perfectly good. The underlying issue is how can evil and suffering exist, if God is both perfectly good and all-powerful? Being all-powerful implies that God has the ability to override evil and suffering. The existence of pain and suffering seems to imply that God is either not all-powerful or not perfectly good.

The most common way, at least in Christian thought, to over-come this dilemma, is to argue that God who is good permits evil and suffering in order to sustain the greater good of human free will. Love, for example, if it is meaningful, is an act of a free will. Love is a choice to make. Therefore, authentic love between us could not exist without free will. Generally, those persons and reli-gions that place a high value on free will argue that God does not will evil in people's lives, but that suffering is a result of free human choices and that people bear the painful consequences of those evil choices.

Another answer is that we live in a corrupt world because of the sin of mankind as evidenced by the story of Adam in the Bible. The "fallen" human condition is prominent in Jewish, Christian, and Islamic thought.

St. Augustine, in the fifth century, taught that evil does not have ontological reality, that is, some reality that has ultimate standing in the world. If good and evil both exist eternally, then we humans are faced with two gods—one that is good and one that is evil. It is clear within Christianity, Judaism, and Islam that evil does not have ultimate standing. Evil will be overcome. Augustine described evil as the absence of good, just as darkness is the absence of light, and injustice is the absence of justice, and hatred is the absence of love. Evil is not created by God, but when people choose to live outside the framework of God's plan and will for their lives, they become evil. Pain and suffering are the outcome of trying to live in the "Garden" without reference to God's presence. Evil, then, is real, but it is not eternal. One of the problems with the notion of an eternal hell turns out to be that it points to the existence of an eternal realm of suffering that God never overcomes.

In Hinduism, suffering is the karmic result of previous lives. In other words, suffering is the reaping of what we sow. Evil will not ultimately prevail. In Buddhism, evil is not an external force but something we create by being focused on selfish craving and self-gratification.

Every world religion struggles with the issue of evil and suffering. While differing faiths address these problems in widely different ways, all our religions hold the problem of evil and suffering in common. Creating open conversations about how our faiths understand and cope with evil can become the fertile soil of meeting one another as serious and devoted people of faith. Our goal should rarely be to achieve intellectual agreement. Our goal should be to listen and learn and to foster mutual respect.

4. *A fourth common thread is that every world religion is characterized by sacred places, holy moments, and sacred literature.* The call to Abraham was a holy moment. The baptism of Jesus was a holy moment. The recitation of God's speaking for humankind was a holy moment. The enlightenment of the Buddha was a holy moment. All our religions hold certain spaces or places to be sacred. The burning bush for Moses was holy ground. The Kaabah in Mecca is regarded as a holy place, as are the Jewish, Christian, and Muslim places of worship in Jerusalem. The Buddhist, Hindu, Daoist temples are holy places. Each of our faiths embraces sacred literature, from the Bhagavad-Gita to the Qur'an to the Old and New Testaments to the Analects and Daodejing.

Sacred places and sacred literature and the celebration of sacred moments belong to all our religious journeys. The existence of the sacred moments and places becomes a platform for building conversations. The heart and soul of effective conversation do not lie in passionate speaking; they lie in active listening. Listening speaks louder than words and proclaims more eloquently than words ever can that every person matters. Listening itself can become a sacred moment.

If we want to build communities of conversation that raise the level of mutual trust among peoples of the world, we should take seriously the voices, the places, and the literature that enlighten and hearten the spirit of diverse believers. We should visit one another's sacred places, the sanctuaries where we shed our grief and gain encouragement for a new day. We should read one another's sacred literature and sense its power to inspire and to instruct. We should listen deeply to the moments that have become sacred, moments that have transformed people's lives.

Listening and learning of the sacred mysteries that lie near the soul of all our faiths will enable us to build bridges of understanding that can reveal to us a better way forward.

5. *A fifth common thread is that all our religions have to deal with the crippling partisanship that scrambles our faiths.* It is a common thread. Some are literalists; some are mystics. Some are moderate or liberal; some are fundamentalists. All our faiths face intense internal assaults—great gulfs of misunderstanding and conflict that cripple the power of a faith's witness and undermine the integrity and authority of religious devotion.

Insofar as our religious organizations are able to begin conversations across the boundaries of belief, those conversations can become the framework for reducing the warring within our religious orders. In the larger world of religious devotion, the differences among Baptists, Methodists, and Presbyterians becomes trivial when we engage in trying to understand the Buddhist way. Our internal warring within our faiths—Shia versus Sunni, Protestant versus Roman Catholic, Therayana versus Mahayana—result from excessive focus on a particular dimension of faith. The feuds between literalists and mystics distort belief.

After all, our religions are human. They are imperfect renderings of spiritual insight. By crossing over the boundaries among our faiths, we are forced to reach back for the inspiring touch-stones of our own religious convictions. Speaking across boundaries, instead of weakening our faith, can serve to strengthen our commitments, not because we become more hardened and rigid, but because we can understand our faith more clearly in relation to the larger context of human community. Refusing to discuss and explore our beliefs with those who differ from us does not protect us; it exposes us to the danger of a shallow religious commitment. A faith of which we cannot speak clearly is a faith that we are not likely to take seriously. Thoughtful, willful conversation among peoples of different faiths lifts us from the mire of internal conflicts that debilitate belief, weaken the power of witness, and consume our energies.

Our internal warring is selfish and unproductive, and, in the final analysis, cowardly. It is so for Christianity, Judaism, Islam, Buddhism, and all other families of faith. If we can find the courage to reach out to one another, we will become less inclined to become absorbed by our own trivial and self-serving disputes.

6. *A sixth common thread is compassion.* In her compelling work, *The Great Transformation,* Karen Armstrong outlines a spiritual revolution in which the currents of yearning for peace and compassion rise to prominence in each of the world religions and cultures. In their highest moments, the world's faiths place the abandonment of self-centered ways and the embrace of a life of compassion at the center of their understanding of what it means to follow God or to be fully human.

The centrality of compassion becomes hidden amongst the caverns of religious hierarchy and ritual. Over and over again, the practices of the faithful become distracted from the heart of faith to the peripheral evidences of being faithful. Demonstrating faithfulness through the external exercises of belief, whether attending worship, participating in religious ritual, or making symbolic sacrifices often trumps the more essential components of being faithful by relating with compassion, by acting to forgive, or by becoming an agent of peace in the world.

Therefore, the centrality of compassion too often becomes obscured. It is obscured by politics in which compassion seems to be a naïve capitulation to authority and power. Compassion is even obscured in religion where it often appears to be a hopelessly impractical ideal. In politics and religion, the ruling powers compete for center stage and their competition belies the efficacy of love and compassion. Being graceful appears weak. As a result, we become quarrelsome instead of loving, power-seeking instead of grace-bearing.

In reality, of course, compassion is not a naïve alternative to hostility and violence. It is a very practical alternative. Compassion leads us to a disciplined, sometimes difficult, dialogue where we seek an alternative to killing or putting other people down because of their beliefs. Compassion requires more intellectual rigor than either prejudice, rejection, or aggression. Aggression and prejudice are intellectually lazy. Pursuing thoughtful, nonviolent compassion requires both intellectual rigor and mindful patience in which we recognize and affirm the worth of other people even when we genuinely disagree with them. Thus, compassion becomes a way forward that is both practically more productive and intellectually more challenging than high-handed religious assertiveness that concedes no value to the beliefs of others. As Christians, the refusal to act with compassion toward other believers remains a testament that we do not believe our own beliefs. If we do not listen with integrity, our proclamations have come loose from the moorings of our own convictions.

Both the idea of compassion and the exercise of disciplined compassion can become one of the common threads around which we weave our conversations and begin the hard work of building bridges.

7. *A seventh thread with which our conversations of faith might be woven is that all of our faiths provide their followers with a pathway of hope.* This pathway of hope may be regarded as salvation or deliverance or liberation. The pathway may lead toward the prospect of a heavenly bliss or release from the burdens and pains of ordinary earthly existence. The pathway of hope may be in finding enlightenment, becoming one with the Brahman or living in harmony with the divine order. In every case, our religions offer the believer a higher and better way of life that will yield a sense of well-being and ultimate happiness. We do not have a consistent notion of heaven and hell that reaches throughout the world of belief, but we do have a universally held confidence in a better way and a higher purpose that will bring meaning and joy to believers. All our faiths find that our ordinary lives are fractured, broken, and twisted. Human sorrow and despair pervade the human family, and faith brings relief and hope to people who live in the grips of pain and fear.

This hope of salvation, however broadly salvation is defined, is one of the universal characteristics of religious devotion. In certain cases, including some adherents to Christianity, the descriptions of an ultimate hell become a further incentive to believe. Christians are sometimes told, for example, that unless they believe in Jesus and accept him as their savior, they are doomed to spend eternity in a fiery abyss. In contrast, the acceptance of Jesus as Lord and Savior, insures that upon death the convert will be ushered into an eternal life of bliss and heavenly reward. All sins are cast away. Other faiths, such as Hinduism, seem more convinced that while the faithful will eventually achieve a universe of selfless bliss, it will only be achieved after repeated incarnations in which adherents, for better or worse, live in the next life the harvest of their present life. In this fashion, individuals grow toward "heaven" through repeated lifetimes until they find their way toward a less egocentric way of living and ultimately become one with the God within.

Many religions also struggle with the disjunction between "believing right" and "behaving right." While neither believing nor behaving should be diminished, belief is too often viewed as an intellectual exercise, and behavior is too frequently identified with a specific human action. The idea of "relating" may become a more powerful and constructive category for explaining both our religious differences and our commonalities. Each of the world's religions changes what it means to relate to the world and to one another. Our faith commitments transform not only our intellectual beliefs or our external behavior; they transform every relationship of life. Relating transcends believing and behaving.

Exploring our divergent pathways of hope can become one common thread around which we can weave a new fabric of understanding among the families of faith. Every person lives in search of hope. Every religion, if it is to endure, must bring a sense of hope to all those who have embraced the faith. Hope is a universal human longing and our common yearning for hope and salvation can become a foundation for building a community of conversation. Listening earnestly and speaking honestly will create a community of conversation that can bring light to all peoples of faith.

14

The Hope for a Greater Reformation

Building bridges could become the foundation for creating a new and greater reformation in a world of devout but diverse believers. For Christians, the Reformation of the sixteenth century was an important step for a church that had lost its way amidst the rising distortions of belief within institutional religion.

While we may hope that Islam will experience a global reformation similar to that experienced by Christianity, there are few parallels between the challenges facing the Muslim faith and those challenges that faced the Roman Catholic Church in the sixteenth century. The Protestant Reformation in Christianity was about the corruption of the Roman Church that obscured the simplicity of grace as the heart of the Christian gospel. Candor also requires that we acknowledge that even though the Christian Reformation was an important corrective, it did not cure all the ills of Christianity. The great Islamic challenge is between warring factions, chiefly the Shia and the Sunni and especially the intersection of Islam with the modern world. This intersection with the modern world may be Islam's greatest challenge. It is not constructive to sit back and simply hope for reform within the individual religions of the world, our own included. Surely greater reforms among all our faiths are needed. We all have much to learn and new spiritual growth to achieve. But I believe that we need to stretch our minds and spirits and raise our expectations further toward even more radical change. Civilization and religion yet remain in an era of adolescence.

Today, we should reach for a new and greater reformation that enables us to transcend the boundaries of our divergent beliefs. The dark era of religious conflict and the human evil those conflicts have spawned can be redeemed, ultimately, only if we are willing to listen to a higher calling to live beyond the narrow confines of our limited religious experiences. History is, I believe, setting the stage for a new and greater reformation.

It is possible, though certainly not inevitable, that the present period of conflict could become the platform from which we are able to achieve a new covenant among the religions of the world. Doing so will require bold and courageous action among people of belief. It will require thoughtfulness and patience; it will require meditation and silence.

In our cultural development as human beings, religion has typically served as a very conservative force, resisting changes and conserving established mores as a moral imperative. The bent toward conserving culture in the name of faith has played a valuable role in human social development. As individual mores have shifted, religion has provided an anchor that keeps society from chasing after every new ideology. Religion has helped to preserve stability and order in the midst of the inevitable chaos of change. The downside to this conservative inclination is that religion very often fails to be a leader in pushing or pulling us toward a higher human order. While religion has helped to conserve the advances of civilization, it has not generally been a leading or constructive voice in the evolution of civilization to a higher level.

In our own country, we saw the effects of cultural conservatism in religious clothing in the vigorous defense of slavery in the middle of the nineteenth century. That conservative inclination reappeared as a resisting force in the South in the dismantling of segregation in the middle of the twentieth century.

I grew up in the racial turmoil of the South and gained a visceral sense of this resistance. Being raised in the South, I had accepted with little question the system of segregation. I participated personally and emotionally in the struggle to shed ourselves of the prejudices that were as natural as the breaking of day. Walking from darkness into light is not an easy journey. It never is. Most of us did not adhere to the system of segregation out of meanness or hostility. This twisted human system was "the way things were." The system simply went unquestioned by the great majority of the majority. When the awful truth of the moral corruption of the system became exposed and we had to face into our own immoral behavior, the first reaction was to be defensive and protective of the status quo. The system seemed to be working just fine for us white folk. But the mask of our self-righteous prejudice soon began to unravel, and we were left naked before our own immorality.

The white Christian church was, in fact, little help. Prophetic voices were rarely heard, but the black Christian church became an eloquent and prophetic voice in dismantling the system. The black church provided both courage and comfort. The black preachers were dismissed as "radical" and labeled as "rabble-rousers" and "troublemakers." Trouble, indeed, they made. It turned out to be holy trouble. The majority white churches mostly resisted the change, only to find themselves offering apologies decades later. More often than not, our Christian churches have been victims of the culture, and that reality works against the tide of reformation. Every world religion has apologies to make.

Our bent is toward preserving the status quo. Religion may have inhibited the development of the cultural and social equality of women, especially in Christianity and Islam. Today, our world's religions are seen far too often to be the handmaidens of nationalistic will. We too often appear to identify Christianity with Western supremacy. Muslims too often appear to identify Islam with Arabic supremacy. Jews too often appear to identify Judaism with supremacy in "the Promised Land." At times, all of us forget that living as the people of the promise is not about the land or the doctrine, but living with mercy, doing justice, and embodying God's spirit.

While in the movement of history the tide of change and reformation can be slowed, it cannot be stemmed. We find vivid examples in all of the world's religions where a remnant of voices see and proclaim a higher and better way. The prophets of the Old Testament are voices crying out against the allegiances to a corrupt and immoral culture, calling for Israel to follow Yahweh and to turn away from their surrender to cultural values and foreign gods. The prophets were pushing against the ruling religious majority that had been subsumed and controlled by the culture. Jesus was a prophetic voice, seeking to refocus Judaism on the reliable, redemptive, and unconditional love of God. Muhammad called bands of disparate Arabian nomadic warring clans into a community of persons submitting themselves to Allah first and foremost. Many imams are calling Muslims away from violence. Pope John Paul XXIII pried open the doors of the Roman Catholic Church to become more open to the faith of non-Catholics. Pope Benedict XVI has opened the doors for conversations with the Muslims. Martin Luther King, Jr. challenged the church and the culture to face up to the evils of segregation and to live up to the truth that all children, black and white, are God's children. We sometimes find God's voice silenced by the majority and heard through a marginalized minority.

The problem with becoming the established religious majority is that we generally stop listening. We have heard God, and whether Muslim, Christian, Jew, or Buddhist, we have developed an elaborate religious machine to demonstrate it and to preserve our vision for posterity. But when we stop listening out for God's centering voice and we turn away from the intensity of God's new and often uncomfortable light, our religious enterprises begin to wither and decay.

Creating new communities of conversation can enable us to take a new and bold step in the evolution and the reformation of the world's great religions. As religious people, we have advanced dramatically from the animistic gods of our primitive forebearers. We have moved beyond the anthropomorphic images of God among the Greek pantheon of gods and the myths of Persia. In our own religious heritage as Christians, Jews, and Muslims, we have climbed to higher levels of insight. Still, we are in our religious infancy. If we are to be faithful, we must continue to mature. Our gathering together, heart to heart and mind to mind, as members of diverse faiths can become the schoolhouse in which we learn new lessons from God and gain better light by which to live. I am not speaking here of theoretical conversations. People from actual congregations of diverse believers need to come together to listen and to pray and to care for one another.

Nothing is more telling of our religious infancy than our barbarous behavior that takes place under the guise of religious devotion. Killing in the name of God, whether by Jews or Christians or Muslims, is barbaric, immoral, and contrary to the character of God. Overcoming this misunderstanding of God's creative and redemptive character and this abuse of religion will require a new and greater reformation.

Transforming our religious priorities and reaching for a higher order of religious understanding will require both greater intelligence and a deeper moral sensitivity. We are still living amidst the chaos. We are living as much in the shadows as in the light. Members of the human race continue to behave toward one another and toward all creation in an uncivilized and immoral manner. The confluence of religion and fear inevitably transforms religion into a tool of incivility and evil. The very survival of human civilization requires that we no longer settle for religious hostility as a righteous way to behave. Our weapons have become so lethal and the combination of zealotry and weapons that are massively destructive poses greater dangers than we have ever faced.

While the dangers are great and the ominous clouds of demonic design remain on the horizon, I believe that we also face the prospects of a new era dawning among mankind and among our religions. Though wars will surely not disappear, I believe that the people of the earth are becoming increasingly unsettled with war as the way to solve human disputes. It is not working. The advance of civilization and the maturing of religion move at a slow pace in human time. Change occurs in centuries and thousands of years. But we are entering an era in which there is mounting evidence that a growing number of the citizens of earth believe there is a better way. Even in totalitarian cultures, voices of dissent are rising more boldly. Reformed and respectful voices of faith can help lead us toward a better way and a higher order of human civilization.

The world is presently undergoing dramatic changes in the way humans connect and in our ability to actually manage the future course of human development. Human beings are in a different place than they have ever been. The human capacity to innovate, to invent, to create, to reimagine ourselves and the world will change the face of humanity. We would be naïve, even foolish, to think that the massive upheavals taking place in human communication (communication that is about far more than sending verbal messages), the expansion of human intelligence, and the rapid advances in the genetic sciences will not affect our religious and spiritual lives. We should hope that religion will not simply be a force to resist change but to guide that change and to take on the moral task of guiding human development toward a higher moral and spiritual understanding.

We are arguably, I believe, in the early stages of the next great leap in the evolution of human life and the concurrent development of human religion. As human beings, we are now creating networks of thought, imagination, and knowledge that will surely change how the human mind works and how human civilization unfolds. Communication, as an enhanced capacity for human connectivity, is blurring the lines among cultures. Ideas and movements no longer have geographic boundaries, and political boundaries are becoming far more porous. People are not only citizens of a nation; they are citizens of the world.

Human imagination is bursting through the limits of understanding. Human intelligence will be able to increase at warp speeds, changing the equation for how people remake the world and creating new paradigms of human interaction. Nations can no longer act politically, economically, or religiously in an isolated fashion. People either connect or they become irrelevant. We either connect our minds and our intellectual capacities or we remain ignorant. We either connect our faiths or we will remain blind.

We should be fascinated with the endgame of Google, which is to bring together and to make accessible to every human mind all the knowledge that exists in the world. And they are close. The goal is not to have a giant library in the World Wide Computing Cloud. The explicit goal is to create artificial intelligence.

In the next one hundred years, the "machines" will know far more than we and will know the questions in our minds before we ask them. These same seeds of dramatic change may be seen in the mapping of the human genome. We will indeed be able and we certainly will manipulate the genetic make-up of human life. From birth, we will be able to treat potential diseases before they occur. I am confident that genetic developments and the manipulations of human biology will create startling changes in human life on earth in the next 150 years. The pace of change, the potential progress and potential destruction are accelerating at mind-bending rates. While all of these developments seem a bit unsettling and will be fraught with enormous and complex ethical challenges, the advance of human development, and in its wake, the development of human civilization, is inexorable.

The world's religions too must advance, and they should help to lead civilization's advance. Creation is still underway. The hope of mankind lies not in resisting the forces of human and religious evolution. Our hope lies in embracing them and guiding them in developing a higher human order. The advancing power of human and extrahuman intelligence will augment the capacity of the human mind. Our greatest challenge as people of faith will be to enable the human race to achieve a heightened moral capacity commensurate with our growing intellectual capacity. We should not be content to become a world of intellectual giants and moral and religious infants.

We can fuel the development of our moral capacity by learning from one another's religious insights. The time is past when we should have begun tearing down walls and building bridges. We must find ways to end our endless disputes and begin to listen and to learn of God from one another. To be sure, the issue for the next great leap of the human species into a higher order of civilization will not likely be simply about whether we know enough. Achieving a higher order will certainly not depend on whether we have developed weapons lethal enough to destroy the planet. Our knowledge and our intelligent manipulation of knowledge are growing rapidly. Our military might is truly extraordinary. The issue is not whether we are intelligent or militarily strong enough, but whether we are good enough. The issue is whether our moral quotient can rise at a pace commensurate to the rise of our intelligence quotient and our power quotient.

Intelligence and might without advancing morality will cause us ultimately to spiral downward as a human civilization. Our greatest challenges may not be intellectual; more likely, they will be moral. The challenge of faith, including our faith as Christians, is to open ourselves to grow to a new level of spiritual insight and, through that insight, to become good enough and wise enough to guide the use of our growing intellectual power to the high purpose of serving God's creative and redemptive presence on earth.

Creating a greater reformation should not be construed as the need for creating a new religion, a religion that would transcend other religions. In my judgment, that would be a mistaken vision. Such an effort would be unlikely to advance either religion or civilization. It would simply become a cauldron for more quarrels. We can do better. We need to create a new relationship among our faiths, a relationship based upon working together to achieve a higher and better human order. All our religions will become better by becoming less consumed by our own individual self-interests. Defensive religious postures and practices are self-defeating because they are egocentric and bent upon self-promotion.

The truth is that all our religions are broken vessels. That reality has caused some people to become absolutely evangelical in their rejection of all religion altogether. Atheism turns out to be only one more form of fundamentalism. Religions are broken because civilization is broken. Our brokenness is a sign of our infancy. Children break things. Look at the human race. We are immature and the question is whether we are prepared to grow up, to begin to behave in ways more civilized, ways that combine civility with respect and combine justice with compassion. I believe we can and will reach for a higher human order. While such an affirmation may sound naïve, I believe it is the trajectory of a creation that is still underway. Only the long look will give us hope.

We will be developing new tools. We will have the capacity to know more and to behave better. Seriously religious people will need to listen to one another more genuinely and replace the passion to convert with a new passion to embrace. We must be willing to share the light we have seen and, together, open ourselves to God's continuing light of creation and redemption.

Though we should not create new religions, we should create new religious language, language that is less exclusive and less judgmental. Our language will become a clue to a new way of relating. The greater reformation, for example, will claim the power of women to model a new way of being in the world. We have barely walked outside the seminal garden of creation. And we have a long journey to arrive at God's land of promise. It is indeed a land where we will beat our swords into plowshares and prepare new wineskins for the new wine of greater human intelligence and wider human and religious embrace. We can change our ways and rewrite our human story. We can be a part of making a new creation in which God speaks to us in many tongues and through many faiths. God, who is not a Christian or a Jew or a Muslim or a Hindu, is the one spirit and the one light that can bring hope to all our faiths and bring hope to our human civilization that embodies the good creation we were destined to become.

For the sake of all humankind, we need a new awakening, a new reformation, a new creation whereby our religious embrace becomes wider and our vision of God's presence becomes richer. Perhaps even now, God is brooding and hovering over the chaos created by conflicting faiths and speaking the creative word within us, "Let there be light." Our common calling as members of the world's faiths is to become instruments of light in a world where the demonic forces of darkness that perpetuate themselves even in the environs of belief threaten to turn out the lights. God's grace enlightens us all. Only the God above all our gods can light our path so that we can live beyond despair toward hope and human redemption.

FOR FURTHER READING

Rollin Armour, Sr., *Islam, Christianity, and the West, a Troubled History* (2002)

Karen Armstrong, *The Great Transformation: The Beginning of Our Religious Traditions* (2006)

Nels Ferré, *The Living God of Nowhere and Nothing* (1966)

R. Kirby Godsey, *When We Talk about God, Let's Be Honest* (1996; repr. 2006)

Warren Matthews, *Abraham Was Their Father* (1981)

J. B. Phillips, *Your God Is Too Small* (1952, 2004)

Irshad Manji, *The Trouble with Islam Today* (2003)

Hans Küng, *Tracing the Way* (2002)

Is God a Christian?